HOLLYWOOD'S
DARK HISTORY

HOLLYWOOD'S DARK HISTORY

SILVER SCREEN SCANDALS

Matt MacNabb

PEN & SWORD **HISTORY**

AN IMPRINT OF PEN & SWORD BOOKS LTD.
YORKSHIRE – PHILADELPHIA

First published in Great Britain in 2019 by
PEN AND SWORD HISTORY
An imprint of
Pen & Sword Books Ltd
Yorkshire – Philadelphia

ISBN 978 1 52674 074 8

Typeset in Times New Roman 12/17 by
Aura Technology and Software Services, India
Printed and bound in the UK by TJ International

Pen & Sword Books Limited incorporates the imprints of Atlas,
Archaeology, Aviation, Discovery, Family History, Fiction, History,
Maritime, Military, Military Classics, Politics, Select, Transport, True
Crime, Air World, Frontline Publishing, Leo Cooper, Remember When,
Seaforth Publishing, The Praetorian Press, Wharncliffe Local History,
Wharncliffe Transport, Wharncliffe True Crime and White Owl.

For a complete list of Pen & Sword titles please contact
PEN & SWORD BOOKS LIMITED
47 Church Street, Barnsley, South Yorkshire, S70 2AS, England
E-mail: enquiries@pen-and-sword.co.uk
Website: www.pen-and-sword.co.uk

Or
PEN AND SWORD BOOKS
1950 Lawrence Rd, Havertown, PA 19083, USA
E-mail: Uspen-and-sword@casematepublishers.com
Website: www.penandswordbooks.com

Contents

Acknowledgements

I would like to first and foremost thank my amazing, beautiful and blissfully intelligent life partner, best friend and wife, Holly MacNabb. Also, my lovely children, Sebastian, Anastasia, Alexandre and Callidora – you four are the light of my life.

I would also like to thank Claire Hopkins for her fantastic patience and for providing me the opportunity to write and research another sliver of history. Also, everyone at Pen and Sword that had any part in the design, editing and proofing of this book – your efforts are all very appreciated.

Finally, I would like to thank you, the reader. I cannot tell you what it means that you are taking valuable time out of your life to read this book. It's an honour and a privilege to be able to curate this for you.

Introduction

Movies are a huge part of the cultural zeitgeist. Film began as a technological novelty, but has evolved over the years into everything from entertainment to education. Movies have become a way for some people to escape their daily lives and become immersed in a fictional reality for a few hours. There are still others that learn from film and those that use it to teach about the past, the present and future of our world. Film has also been used as a propaganda tool at times, intended at conveying a particular reality for the viewing audiences. No matter what movies mean to you, they are undeniably a major part of our lives.

It isn't simply a form of entertainment either, movies can truly impact our lives. What some have dismissed at times as mindless has actually been shown to have a positive impact on our collective mental health. In a paper by University of Essex scholar and PhD S.C. Noah Uhrig, titled 'Cinema is Good for You: The Effects of Cinema Attendance on Self-Reported Anxiety or Depression and Happiness', these effects are explored in-depth. In the paper, Uhrig states:

> Cinema attendance can have independent and robust effects on mental wellbeing because visual

stimulation can queue a range of emotions and the collective experience of these emotions through the cinema provides a safe environment in which to experience roles and emotions we might not otherwise be free to experience.

In a world that is constantly in a state of flux, cinema can serve as a snapshot of our past. We can see how our culture has changed dramatically over the years and how our vision of life and the future has been modified. There is also the opportunity for film to inspire us creatively and philosophically about our present and future.

Film allows us to relate to people in a way that we might not have the occasion to do otherwise. In an era when politics are as divisive as ever, and there is so much divide in the world, you can still approach someone and ask if they've seen the latest superhero film or comedy and start up a lively and friendly discussion. There are few topics in the world that have that ability to provide a neutral ground. That discussion can often be a agreeable one, or it can lead to some friendly debate that allows our passions to come to the surface in a healthy and respectful way.

Vaudeville

It was through the experience provided on the vaudevillian stages that provided a nearly seamless transition for many stars onto the silver screen. The origins of vaudeville harken back centuries, but came into immense popularity at the tail-end of the nineteenth century. A growing empire of travelling troupes and theatres had established themselves as the pervasive entertainment venue. They would travel from town to town, entertaining the masses. This was a lovely form of entertainment that has since become a cult favourite for many, but it was only an occasional release from the stresses of daily life. The next step of progression for society would be a more accessible form of entertainment.

Silent Movies

The first movie ever produced was the *Roundhay Garden Scene* in 1888 and consisted of a man riding a horse. It was simple and rudimentary, but it helped to give birth and inspiration to an entire industry. The first true feature-length film that had any sort of content was a military documentary about the training techniques of British soldiers. In 1906, however, we would be given the Australian dramatic feature film, *The Story of the Kelly Gang*. This would launch an industry of silent film that would quickly become a favourite with the public.

The silent film was the birth of the industry. Although it would be relatively short lived, the era of the silent film would launch the careers of a good number of stars that would carry over to the talkies. It would also find many actors that had been brought in for their looks cast aside, due to a thick accent or voices that weren't considered favourable for the screen.

The silent movies brought actors into their homes, made them literally household names. No longer did the public have to just read about these talented individuals or see pictures, but they could actually witness the show for themselves. It became standard place to have a movie theatre in most cities. These buildings served as a great equaliser, where the common person could enjoy comedy, drama and action just the same as the wealthy had been able to do in the theatre.

Film is by no means distinctly American, but it was Hollywood that would end up leading the most prolific charge in the film industry. The migration of young talent that moved across the country from the East coast of New York to California could be likened to a second gold rush, with droves of aspiring actors looking to find their fame and fortunes in an exciting new industry.

Talkies

Silent movies were an amazing progression and created many stars, but it was the advent of the 'Talkie' that would truly change movies forever. Although the techniques were being perfected for many years, it wouldn't be until the mid-1920s that the talking pictures began to take hold and were marketed as the future. The first major film that was a talkie was the 1927 movie, *The Jazz Singer.*

The Silver Screen

The term 'silver screen' refers widely to the movies, but this terminology does have a specific origin. In an effort to help the projected images pop better on the screen, they would literally paint them with a reflective silver or aluminium paint. There were other types of screens used, as well, such as grey screen, pearlescent screens and glass-beaded screens, but the silver screen was the most prolific. The name of these silver lenticular screens would stay with motion pictures as a moniker for the early days of Hollywood.

Hollywood Babylon

Although the studios did a great job of masking the true lives of their stars, the debauchery of the Hollywood elite has come to light over the ages since. We now know, for example, that the studios would encourage their female stars to have abortions. The procedure could be quite dangerous in those days, as it was illegal and often performed by less than qualified individuals in conditions of questionable sanitation. An anonymous actress from the era once touted, 'Abortions were our birth control'. There was also a close monitoring of weight and public behaviour. The studios were very careful to portray their talent in a way that would make them the most marketable to the moviegoing public. The studios would get involved to the point of paying off tabloids and newspapers to keep the content positive towards their talent. This tactic would work for a time, but occasionally the scandals or crimes were just too big to sweep under the rug and they became a subject of national scrutiny.

Hollywood hasn't changed much over the years. The lack of respect for actors and their bodies has carried into the present day. We can hardly tune into the news without learning about another actor or Hollywood bigwig who hasn't abused their power and position to sexually exploit women trying to break into the industry or gain some ground in their career. It isn't just the female actors that are subject to this abuse, there is plenty of talk about similar abuse of male actors that want to get into the business.

Scandal seems to be a given in today's world, as more and more dark and seedy details seep out about our favourite big-screen characters. It can be a former heartthrob that abuses women or a famous producer that turns out to be a serial sexual assaulter. In the case of Bill Cosby, this star of the big and small screen shocked the world, as he was once the friendly and loveable television dad that so many viewers yearned for on his series, *The Cosby Show*. What Cosby represented to the American public was a tough, smart and wholesome father figure. Unfortunately, the reality of Bill Cosby, who has now been convicted of only a fraction of his accused crimes, was a serial rapist. These characters can become so believable to us as an audience that we buy into them and the lines of reality begin to blur. It can be shocking when those barriers are shattered by the real people behind the screen.

When it comes to the stars of yesterday, the black-and-white images of these long-gone glamorous stars can often fool younger audiences into romanticising them. The truth is that these actors of yesterday were just as troubled, if not more so, than the Hollywood crowd of today. This book contains stories widely forgotten, but once uncovered they reveal a dark interior to the glitz and glamour of yesterday.

Introduction

The many subjects in this book had lives that intersected. They were commonly colleagues and contemporaries, but still others were far more involved with each other. There are a few of the scandals that will also intersect, and certainly Hollywood was a tight-knit community comprised of many friends and companions. I sincerely hope that you find enjoyment, education and perspective in these sensational tales of lies, murder and violence from the golden age of Hollywood.

Chapter One

Evelyn Nesbit

She was born Florence Evelyn Nesbit on 25 December 1884, but she would be best known by her middle name, Evelyn. Her long and illustrious life began in a small Pennsylvania town called Tarentum. Situated along the Allegheny River, Tarentum was an industrial town, focusing on iron and lumber manufacturing. The blue-collar area isn't known for many famous alumni, especially those that would enter the entertainment field. Although it would produce John Grant, a screenwriter for Abbot and Costello, and Estelle Harris, known for her work on the television show *Seinfeld* and the *Toy Story* film franchise. A few movies have been shot in the cosy town, but other than that there isn't much connection with the entertainment industry or the outside world. The most famous, and certainly most infamous, person born from Tarentum was silver-screen legend Evelyn Nesbit. She was the most recognisable face in America at one point – and would soon after become the most infamous thanks to a complicated love triangle full of abuse, and eventually murder.

Her Early Life

The life that she and her family led in Tarentum was steeped in poverty, but for much of her childhood Evelyn was happy because she had the love of an adoring father. The daughter of Winfield Scott Nesbit and his wife Evelyn Florence (née McKenzie); Evelyn would spend the first seven to nine years of her life in Tarentum before moving to the big city of Pittsburgh. She was the jewel of her father Winfield's eye. Not only was she regarded from birth as a beautiful child, but her father also recognised a bright and eager mind that was more than happy to consume the vast library of books he read to with her as a child. He hoped to help expand and encourage her great creativity and imagination. These are no doubt factors that would play into her future choice of professions. Evelyn would later recount of her childhood, 'In my young mind I turned the grim realities into a wonderland where I might roam'. She had moments where she dared to dream of fame and fortune – she would find her fair share of fame in her lifetime.

Alas, her time with her father would be cut short, as he died suddenly when Evelyn was at the pivotal age of 11. This would change the course of Evelyn's life, because it would leave the family destitute. Her mother did everything from turning their home into a boarding house to make ends meet, to selling their furniture to pay the rent. The family would often have to survive on just bread and mustard for their meals. Evelyn would have to travel between boarding houses, while her mother looked tirelessly for work. The kids would spend time being sent away to various relatives and friends to live, as was a common practice in that time.

In 1899 the family moved to Philadelphia where their mother would find work at Wanamaker's department store. When Evelyn was 14 her mother sent for her and her

2

younger brother and they would be reunited as a family. The trio all served as employees for Wanamaker's, working long twelve-hour days, six days per week. Her mother was so intent on the kids working with her at the department store that she is said to have lied about Evelyn's birth year, so some theorise she was actually born in 1886. The family could still barely get by financially, even with their combined salaries. The time that Evelyn spent at the department store would change her life and create a legend.

A Model is Born

> When I saw I could earn more money posing as an artist's model than I could at Wanamaker's, I gave my mother no peace until she permitted me to pose for a livelihood.
>
> Evelyn Nesbit

One fateful day when Evelyn was hard at work, she had a chance encounter with an artist that became instantly enamoured with the beauty and grace of the teen and asked her to model for one of her paintings. Her mother agreed, since the artist was a woman and it presented no danger for her child. The sitting earned Evelyn $1, which translates to around $27 today (approximately £21). Feeling strongly that this easier way of making money was for her over retail work, she pushed her mother to allow her to obtain more modelling work, and that is just what she did. She became an instant hit with the Philadelphia art community and was able to find many jobs posing for photography and portraits alike. Unfortunately, this age of prosperity for Evelyn and her family soon came to an end as her mother attempted to relocate to New York in 1900. She was a seamstress by trade and was looking for work in that field. Unfortunately, her attempts to find work were unsuccessful and when she finally sent for her children to join her, their financial situation was yet again in ruins. Fortunately for the Nesbits, a number of the Philadelphia artists had written letters of recommendation for Evelyn to their contacts in New York, so she was able to easily find work again there as a model.

Mrs Nesbit would become a sort of makeshift manager of Evelyn's career, but unfortunately she was far from fit to handle the role. She wasn't very well-versed in the business of modelling. Evelyn's mother was never able to take her career seriously or expel the energy required to truly manage her well. On top of that, what Evelyn perhaps needed the most at her young age was a proper chaperone, which her mother also wasn't able to accomplish, despite her own assertions that she was. During her teen years Evelyn would end up posing nude – something that was quite a scandal.

Despite her mother's ineptitude, Evelyn's career soared, with her gracing ads in the pages of *Ladies' Home Journal*, *Vanity Fair*, *Cosmopolitan* and *Harper's Bazaar* among others. Her face became a commonplace standard and she may have even been the very first pin-up girl. Evelyn was the most photographed woman of her era by the time she was just 16 years old.

Her beauty and delicacy were so much that she was used as one of the models for illustrator Charles Gibson's famous 'Gibson Girls'. Gibson defined the feminine ideal through his art for a solid two decades in the United States and Canada. His designs first appeared in the 1890s as a depiction of the 'fragile lady' that was a part of society and, while slender and tall, also had a curvy physique. One of his best known works, 'Woman: The Eternal Question', was based on her.

Evelyn Meets Stanford White

Stanford White was a legend in New York City. He was a partner in the architectural firm McKim, Mead & White. It's difficult to imagine the city without his designs, as he was a highly gifted architect. The structures that White erected captured the imagination of all. Stanford is responsible for designing some iconic structures, like the Washington Square Arch, Madison Square Garden, the Rhode Island State House, Tiffany and Company's Building and even the Omaha National Bank.

Stanford was a devout workaholic, determined to be constantly designing and fully realising his gifts. He would often juggle dozens of projects at a time. His passion for all things beautiful drove him in his work. What wasn't widely known at the time is that the man behind these genius structures was a professional master, but a personal monster.

A series of bad investments had left Stanford broke years before he met Evelyn, but he kept on spending like nothing had happened, believing that he should live better than his clients. He would have parties at his lovely penthouse apartment. Evelyn began attending these parties and Stanford took an instant liking to her. Evelyn would comment that she found him to be old and somewhat repulsive, but that he was of good temperament. The two would become firm friends, with Stanford being a gentlemen in her presence, even taking her up to the roof at night to look at the wonders of the city.

Evelyn's mother, ever the purveyor of good decisions, was thrilled that a rich benefactor had taken notice of her daughter. It was assumed that he was taking her under his wing to care for her like a daughter, but that was not the case. Stanford soon moved the family out of the boarding house they were staying in and into a lovely hotel, where he paid their bills. Evelyn's mother so trusted White that she felt comfortable going back home to visit relatives, leaving Evelyn under his care. This time would come to shape her life.

White took Evelyn on a special photo shoot with a photographer friend of his. He adorned her in Japanese kimonos from his personal collection. He mused with his friend that her mother had left her in his care, and the two shared a laugh about this. The full details of what happened next were unknown to the world until the trial of her future husband – Harry Thaw. Evelyn would confide in Thaw that White drugged and raped her, taking her virginity.

Evelyn and Harry Thaw

Evelyn was able to make her way onto Broadway, where the wealthy men would adorn the actresses and chorus girls with gifts and attention. She debuted in a Broadway musical titled *Florodora*, with a small role as a Spanish dancer. She would gain the attention of many wealthy men, including Harry Thaw, the son of a railroad speculator.

Harry Thaw began sending her roses under the guise of 'Mr Monroe'. He was an awkward man, infamous for his violent mood swings. The patrons in the Broadway district called him 'Mad Harry'. He had a notoriety for outlandish stunts, like lighting his cigars with $100 bills. There were stories of him utilising violence in the past. A woman by the name of Ethel Thomas sued him for $20,000 in 1902 for allegedly taking her to a Fifth Avenue building and whipping her repeatedly.

Thaw lived his life of luxury and parties in the public eye – at least on most days. He would also have secret hideaways where less savoury acts would go on. There would be private parties with women there for 'entertainment'. During this era there was a movement against immorality in New York City. Those involved in this new movement were determined to reform the idea that these rich, married men would constantly cheat on their wives and engage in negative business practices. President Theodore Roosevelt spoke out against these business practices, emboldening a major movement: The New York Society for the Suppression of Vice, led by Anthony Comstock. The Society got a report from Thaw that White was using hideaways to drug underage girls. Thaw, who became obsessed with White and the behaviour he had seen, calculated that over 300 girls had been victimised by White – their virginity stolen.

During this time, Thaw was trying desperately to woo Evelyn and gain her favour. She soon fell seriously ill and Thaw was very attentive to her, helping to get surgery and bring her back to health afterwards. He sent Evelyn and her mother to Europe, so that she could have time to recover. He soon followed and they spent time together in Paris, Thaw lavishing her with gifts and attention. This was a perfect way for Thaw to isolate her from White's influence, which was never ending in New York.

Thaw began discussing marriage with Nesbit while they were in Paris. She tried her best to pass him off, but he pushed the idea aggressively. It was there in Paris, one fateful evening, that Evelyn revealed her lengthy sexual affair with White – a seemingly consensual affair that had begun only after he had drugged and raped her while she was unconscious. This enraged Thaw, who already had ill-will towards White for this behaviour. The idea that White had harmed Evelyn consumed him.

Thaw quickly separated Evelyn from her mother on the trip. Evelyn and Harry travelled on to Holland and various locations in Germany, travelling as husband and wife the whole time, though they were not married. Eventually, they would arrive at the Schloss-Katzenstein in Austria. Thaw had rented out an entire end of the for their stay. It was while they were there that the abuse began.

Evelyn would soon return to New York, where she ran to Stanford White for help. White immediately took Evelyn to his lawyer to make a statement. Nesbit recounted the events in her statement to White's lawyer:

> After breakfast the said Thaw said he wished to tell me something and asked me to step into my bedroom. I entered the room, when the said Thaw, without any provocation, grasped me by the throat and tore the bath-robe from my body. I saw by his face that the said Thaw was in a terrific excited

condition, and was terrorized. His eyes were glaring and he had in his right hand a cowhide whip. He seized hold of me and threw me on the bed. I was powerless and attempted to scream, but the said Thaw placed his fingers in my mouth and tried to choke me.

He then, without any provocation, and without the slightest reason, began to Inflict on me severe and violent blows with the cowhide whip. So brutally did he assault me that my skin was cut and bruised. I besought him to desist, but he refused. I was so excited that I shouted and cried. He stopped every minute or so to rest, and then renewed his attack upon me, which he continued for about seven minutes.

He acted like a demented man. I was absolutely in fear of my life. The servants could not hear my outcries for the reason that my voice did not penetrate through the large castle, and so could not come to my succcor [sic]. The said Thaw threatened to kill me, and by reason of his brutal attack, as I have above described, I was unable to move.

The following morning Thaw again came into my bedroom and administered a castigation similar to the day before. He took a cowhide whip and belaboured [sic] me with it on my bare skin, cutting the skin and leaving me in a fainting condition. I swooned and did not know how long after I returned to consciousness.

This un-merceful [*sic*] beating of the whip left me in a frightfully nervous condition, my fingers very numb, and I was in bodily fear that Thaw would take my life. It was nearly three weeks before I was sufficiently recovered to be able to get out of my bed and walk.

When I did so, the said Thaw took me to a place called Ortler Mountain, where Italy, Switzerland, and Germany conjoin. Then we went into Switzerland. In Switzerland we remained at the Hotel Schweitzerhof, that night at Santa Maria. The next morning I made some remark, and said Thaw took a rattan whip, and while I was in my nightgown, beat me over my leg below the knee so violently that I screamed for help. When I began to scream, the said Thaw again stuffed his fingers in my mouth. During all the time I traveled with the said Thaw, he would make the slightest pretext an excuse for a terrific assault on me. During all this period, my mother continued in London. Thaw and I finally reached Paris about the middle of September, where we occupied apartments at No. 5 Avenue D'Antin. I was constantly watched by detectives and other hirelings of the said Thaw, including his coachman and his valet named Bedford. One day, while in Paris, he assaulted me with a rattan for an entire day, at intervals of half an hour or an hour, striking me severe blows on the body as a result of which I fainted.

Her complaint also revealed that Thaw had developed an addiction to Cocaine:

> One day my maid was in my room, taking things out of the drawers and packing them away. I found a little silver box, oblong in shape, and about two and a half inches long, containing a hypodermic syringe and some other small utensils. I went to the said Thaw and asked him what it was and what it meant, and he then stated to me that he had been ill and tried to make some excuse, saying he had been compelled to use cocaine. I realized then for the first time that the said Thaw was addicted to the cocaine habit. I also frequently saw said Thaw administering cocaine to himself internally by means of small pills. On one occasion he attempted to force me to take one of these pills, but I refused to do so.

Nesbit went to White regarding the abuse. Here was a woman, stuck in a place where, on one side, there was a wealthy madman physically assaulting her to an extreme degree, and the only person she feels she can run to for help is the man that took her virginity by raping her.

She tried to hide from Thaw, but he hired detectives to find her. When the two met up again, she accused him of being unstable, violent and addicted to cocaine. He assured her that he loved her and was devoted to her. His pleas would eventually soften Evelyn and two years later, in 1905, she would agree to marry him. Evelyn is said to have worn black to her own wedding.

The Murder

Stanford White, a 53-year-old architect, would meet his end one fateful evening at the hands of Evelyn's husband Harry Thaw, when Thaw's obsession finally became too much.

The story isn't a new one, but it has been painted in various ways. According to some sources, Thaw was a jealous husband whose wife had had an affair years before with the wealthier, high-society player, Stanford White. According to Nesbit and Thaw, however, the reality is that Stanford White had set the events of that evening in motion himself, six years prior.

Depending on which source you read, the situation is referred to as both a love triangle and an affair, but in truth, the situation between Evelyn Nesbit and Stanford White was a case of a victim rationalising her assault.

Stanford White resided at Madison Square Garden, but the scene of the original crime took place at White's secret hideaway at number 22, 24th Street in New York City. If you walk along the route to the building today you'll find only an empty space between buildings 18 and 24 that serves as a parking lot. Once upon a time it housed a property owned by White. The building was a smaller property, sandwiched in between two vastly taller buildings.

White had seen Nesbit perform on stage and was enamoured with her. He showered her with gifts continuously, until she finally agreed to see him socially. She accompanied him to lunch and then back to his hideaway. We know that what happened next involved White drugging and sexually assaulting the teenage Nesbit. No doubt confused and struggling to deal with the horror that she had experienced, she subsequently began a consensual affair with White.

It was this time in Nesbit's life that her future husband would let rage and the idea of revenge consume him, and commit what would be known at the time as 'the crime of the century'. White was seemingly unaware that Thaw was out to get him, considering him beneath his notice. On 25 June 1906, Mr and Mrs Thaw attended a brand new show at the Madison Square Garden rooftop theatre, titled *Mam'zelle Champagne*. White was in attendance, so Thaw came armed and ready to exact revenge for his beloved and the way she had been treated. He waited until the finale of the show and, as the tenor on stage sang *I Could Love A Million Girls,* he and Evelyn made their way to the elevators in the crowded room. Thaw excused himself from Evelyn and disappeared into the crowd. He re-emerged only 2ft from White, drew his pistol and put three bullets into White's head. He then held his arms aloft and proclaimed, 'I did it because he ruined my wife! He had it coming to him. He took advantage of the girl and then abandoned her! … You'll never go out with that woman again.' Thaw then walked through the crowd, gun still in the air, and met Nesbit back at the elevators. He was eventually taken into police custody and she was left in a state of shock.

The Trials

It was the scandal that shocked a nation. There was so much attention and prying by the press that the twelve-person jury was ordered to be sequestered by the judge. This was a brand new concept and had never been done before in the history of American jurisprudence. The jury was sequestered to keep them from being tainted or tampered with by the immense amount of coverage and nosy members of the press who were desperate to get near the jury.

There wasn't just one trial for Harry Thaw, there were two. The first trial garnered an unprecedented amount attention from the press. It was common for murder trails to get some headline coverage, but this was a murder of a famous and wealthy man by another wealthy man over a beautiful young woman, perhaps the best known and most recognisable woman in America at that time. A propaganda machine funded by the Thaw family fortune immediately went to work creating public sympathy for Harry. The family even hired a public relations representative to write a book: *A Woman's Sacrifice: The Great Harry Thaw Case.* This book would come out after the first trial, telling a story completely slanted in favour of the Thaw family. In their narrative, Thaw was simply a valiant and loving husband defending the honour of his wife. The Thaw family, as Evelyn had noted when living among them for a time after she and Thaw were first married, were overly concerned with appearances.

Postcards and sheet music were released with Thaw's image on them, adorned with phrases like, 'For the Sake of Wife and Home'. Thaw, who lived like a king while waiting in prison for his trial, was absolutely convinced that he would be vindicated on the grounds that he was sticking up for Evelyn. Thaw was far more worried about what the public felt about him than he was about any sort of punishment for his crime.

The first trial began on 23 January 1907 with the public banned from the courtroom. During the trial, Evelyn herself would be asked to recall not only the events at the scene of the crime, but also the nature of her relationship with Thaw and White. It is through her own words that the world learned of what Stanford White did to her, and how he continued to attempt to manipulate her afterwards.

Evelyn would recount the first time she met White and when he drugged and sexually assaulted her:

> The next night, I got a note from Mr White asking me to come down to the studio for luncheon after the theatre with some his friends. A carriage would call for me, and would take me home after the party, he wrote. I went down to the Twenty-fourth street studio again and found Mr White and no one else there. 'What do you think,' he said to me, 'the others have turned us down.' Then I told him I had better go home, and he told me that I had better sit down and have some fruit. So I took off my hat and coat. Mr White told me he had other floors in the garden, and that I had not seen all of his place. He would take me around and show me, he said.
>
> So he took me up some stairs to the floor above, where there were very beautiful decorations. I played for him, and he took me into another room. That room was a bedroom. On a small table stood

a bottle of champagne and one glass. Mr White poured out just one glass for me, and I paid no attention to it. Mr White went away, came back and said: 'I decorated this room, myself.' Then he asked me why I was not drinking my champagne and I said I did not like it; it tasted bitter. But he persuaded me to drink it and I did. A few moments after I had drank it there began a pounding and thumping in my ears and the room got all black. When I came to myself I was greatly frightened and I started to scream. [Evelyn described seeing blood on her thigh and realising that she had had sex.] Mr White came and tried to quiet me. As I sat up I saw mirrors all over. I began to scream again, and Mr White asked me to keep quiet, saying that it was all over. Then he threw the kimono over me he left the room. I screamed harder than ever. I don't remember much of anything after that. He took me home and I sat up all night crying.

Her emotional testimony continued with her relaying how White then made her promise not to tell her mother what had transpired between them. He would laugh and then tell her that there was 'nothing so nice as young girls…'

She would admit to seeing White again after the incident, as he continued to groom her, and even befriended her mother on the pretence that he was acting as a guardian for Evelyn to keep her out of trouble. Once she was with Thaw and had discussed the attack with him, he insisted that she not see or talk to White again. Evelyn recounted

16

one particular day that she ran into White on the street and the fear that consumed her:

> It was on Fifth avenue one day when I was riding to Dr Delavan to have my throat treated. I was in a hansom and Mr White was also riding in a hansom, too. When I got home I told Mr Thaw that at about Thirty-fourth street I had passed Mr White, both of us in hansoms. He did not attempt to speak to me, but stared hard at me. I looked away. When I got down to the doctor's office I found Stanford White in his hansom coming there. I ran up the steps, but I was excited and nervous and I told the door porter that I would come some other time, so I ran back down the stairs, jumped into my hansom, looked neither to the right nor to the left, and told the driver to go back to the Lorraine as quickly as ever he could.

Evelyn was far from White's only victim. There was much discussion in the courtroom about various incidents that White was accused of sexually assaulting various young actresses at the theatre, and even a girl who jumped out of a pie at a stag party he had attended. White was said to have laughed off the incidents when he was confronted with the accusations. Evelyn's testimony painted a vivid picture of a monster who needed to be stopped, a sentiment that she said Thaw supported. He obsessed over her encounter with White and keep close track of White's other interactions and controversies, stating that he should be in a penitentiary.

Anthony Comstock also submitted an affidavit to the trial that detailed his interactions with Thaw in regard to White:

> I know that Stanford White was a human monster. I know that much of what Mrs Harry Thaw has stated as a witness is true. I know that Stanford White's den in the tower of Madison Square garden was as she has described it. I know that White made a business of destroying young girls. I know of at least one specific instance. And what I know I learned after I had been given the first clews [*sic*] by Harry Kendall Thaw himself.
>
> My first knowledge of this case dates from the summer of 1905 – about a year before the killing, I should say. One afternoon a tall, well-dressed, well-bred young man came to me in my office in the Temple Bar building. He seemed to be labouring under excitement, and it was evident that he was desperately in earnest. He opened the conversation by asking me if I were interested in the suppression of vice. Then he wanted to know if my society gave special attention to the arrest and punishment or men who preyed upon young girls. I told him that we did. He jumped up abruptly, said he would see me again, and left without telling me his name. At the door he stopped long enough to say he would see me again.

A few days later he came back, still labouring under strong emotion. He then introduced himself. As nearly as I can recall he said:

'I am Harry Kendall Thaw of Pittsburg. I want to tell you of a man who has betrayed more young girls than any other man in New York. He is particularly given to pursuing the young girls of the stage. It is a debt which society owes to itself to halt him now, before he brings shame and sorrow any more victims.'

That in effect was his statement, although of course I asked him a great deal more of the matter. He left after securing my promise to investigate. He agreed to pay the cost of looking into the case. He at once mailed me a check of sufficient size to defray the necessary expenses, and subsequently wrote me several times upon the subject of White, asking each time what progress we were making.

Our investigation confirmed to a great degree what Thaw had told me. Our detectives were astounded at what they discovered. We worked hard and I learned a great deal, but of all cases these are the hardest to prove under the rules of evidence, and before risking an arrest I determined to catch White.

I learned that his rooms in the tower were as Mrs Evelyn Thaw had described them in the trial. Two of our detectives endeavoured to hire rooms in the same tower in order to watch his goings and comings. The deal was almost completed when one of the detectives made a bungle. Something which he said or did gave the alarm to the janitor, and, although we were on the waiting list for a long time, and although several times apartments in the tower were vacant, we were never able to secure a suite or a single room.

We were still vainly trying to arrange a trap for White from which there would be no escape when he dismantled his room in the tower.

I learned positively of one case of White's conduct to a girl only 15 years old almost identically as Mrs Evelyn Thaw describes her own case, but the girl was in the chorus of a road company, and we could not reach her and make a witness of her. We got evidence of other things – things that convince me that what Harry Thaw's wife now swears is true. I believe in her story and base that belief upon what I know of the man.

Press Coverage

The trial was dubbed by the press as the 'Garden Murder'. The attention from the press was so extreme that the annoyance went all the way to the top. President Theordore Roosevelt himself began to get involved with the circus. Roosevelt consulted the Postmaster General at the time to see if they could restrict the sale of newspapers through the mail service. Roosevelt had also given consideration to censoring the free press. The tradition of the free press as an entity not controlled or restricted by the government has been one celebrated in America since the very beginning of the nation. The idea that the president even considered censoring the news media was shocking and unprecedented.

The headlines across the country went wild, with various newspapers screaming the salacious news. 'Harry Thaw Kills Stanford White On Roof Garden', 'Thaw Goes to Court in Handcuffs', 'New York, 3 P.M. World's Special Service Thaw Jury Has So Far Given No Verdict', 'Jury in Thaw Case Disagrees', 'Thaw Not Guilty On Insanity Ground', 'Was Thaw Justified' and 'Harry Thaw's Choice: Mad House or Death Chair'.

The story was irresistible to the public, because they already looked upon the wealthy as an enemy and something to envy. The wealthy themselves had presented themselves as a type of American royalty, imagining that they were gifted their wealth through the virtue of their characters. In actuality, they were rather predatory and underhanded men – both in business and in their personal lives. In 1906 there were dozens of newspapers in New York City, not just a few like today, so there was a barker on every corner selling the sensational story of one rich man shooting another over a showgirl. It was such a fascinating event that the Biograph Company produced a live action dramatisation of the events within just a week for the murder. It was titled *The Thaw-White Tragedy*. This was in the era where sensational tabloid journalism had taken over, so this trial was just what they needed to sell copy.

In 1906 just 1 per cent of American families controlled 90 per cent of the country's wealth. A good number of these resided in New York City. The rich were living lives of luxury while their employees laboured hard for sixty hours a week and lived in crowded tenement buildings. The divide between the classes was extreme and deeply felt by the hordes of workers who had travelled to New York in search of a new life. The details of this story only amplified this divide, making it a constant interest to those that may not have even known the extent of the level of decadence previously.

The Verdict

The first trial deliberation took forty-seven hours, before the first jury came back deadlocked. There was no verdict for, or against, Thaw. This angered and confused Thaw, who believed his was an open and shut case.

The second trial would begin in January of 1908. This time, instead of going for a temporary insanity plea, the defence strategy turned to outright insanity. Thaw's mother even testified to their family having a history of mental illness. This time, their strategy worked. Thaw was found not guilty by reason of insanity and was sentenced to life incarceration at the Mattewan State Hospital for the Criminally Insane. On his way from the courtroom to the asylum, there were crowds gathered to cheer for Harry.

Thaw is Insane

Harry Thaw may have claimed insanity, but as many wealthy and privileged in society, he was never forced to truly undergo any assistance, or to live in the same way as the other patients. His money would purchase him comforts and treatment that others could not afford. During his time there he fathered a child with Evelyn. She would name him Russell William Thaw.

In a bold move that shows the level of privilege embodied by Thaw, he simply decided that he was tired of being committed, so he escaped in 1913 with financial assistance from his mother. Thaw fled to Quebec, Canada, but was soon extradited back to the United States by the end of 1914. Thaw's lawyer was able to secure him a new trial, where he was found not guilty and declared sane on 16 July 1915. Thaw filed for divorce from Evelyn upon his release. Harry Kendall Thaw was a free man. This situation, however, would not last long.

Thaw went on to abuse more young people, this time turning his attention to a 19-year-old man by the name of Frederick Gump. In 1916 Thaw whipped and raped the boy in a Kansas City hotel room. He had lured him there under the guise that he was going to help him by underwriting his enrolment to the Carnegie Institute. Thaw would offer the Gump family half-a-million dollars to drop the charges, but they ultimately refused. Thaw was apprehended and found insane. This time, he was committed to the Kirkbride Asylum under tight security.

In 1924 Henry Thaw was pushing to be declared sane yet again and to be released from the Pennsylvania Hospital for Mental and Nervous Diseases, where he had been a patient for the prior seven years. Evelyn saw this as a possible detriment to her son, and she fought Harry's release on the grounds that he would undoubtedly squander his fortune upon release. Ultimately, wealth and power won out and Thaw was released.

Film Career and Later Life

Evelyn may have been a famous face before the murder trails, but after that she was infamous. The transition from stage to the Silver Screen came in 1914, when she had a role in *Threads of Destiny*. She would go on to star in eleven feature films, some of those with her son Russell Thaw.

Evelyn is one of the few subjects of this book that actually lived a long and full life. She would eventually pass away in a Santa Monica, California nursing home on 14 January 1967, at the age of 82.

Legacy

Evelyn Nesbit will go down in history as one of the most beautiful and tortured women of her era. She served as the inspiration for Charles Dana Gibson's 'Gibson Girl' ideal and it's no surprise that she continues to engage and enthral audiences to this day. She was one of the most recognisable faces of her generation, but unfortunately her film work didn't leave a lasting impression, so she has yet to enjoy a star on the Hollywood Walk of Fame.

Chapter Two

Thelma Todd

Life

Thelma Alice Todd was born 29 July 1905 to a well-to-do family. Her father, John Shaw Todd, was an active politician and her mother, Alice Elizabeth Edwards, was a housewife. The Todd family was nestled comfortably on the eastern seaboard of the United States in Lawrence, Massachusetts. Her beauty didn't go unnoticed and she began entering pageants as a teenager. Thelma eventually won the crown of Miss Massachusetts in 1925. It was this title that got her noticed by Hollywood. A scout discovered Todd and lured her out west to California for a career in the pictures.

Thelma Todd was a stunning blonde comedian known to many as 'Hot Toddy', or 'The Ice Cream Blonde'. She stands out as one of the few actresses of the time to use her birth name throughout her film career, rather than a screen name.

Early Career

It was silent films that first brought Thelma to worldwide audiences. Her striking looks made her a natural fit for the big screen. Unfortunately, during this era she wasn't given much of a chance to act, but rather serve as a beautiful set-piece in the silent films. She found a good career in the movies, but the comfort of this easier acting life wouldn't last, because sound was about to revolutionise the motion-picture industry.

There were many side effects to the advent of what were then known as 'talkies'. A good number of Hollywood stars were actually foreign and many didn't speak very good English. This language barrier would prevent many stars from crossing over to the new world, as it were. There were still many others that had speech impediments or quite simply weren't great actors when it came to being heard out loud.

Another issue was the way in which a film was made had to change. The actors not only had to have a good vocal presence, but now they needed to memorise their lines in advance and stand still while delivering lines, so that the microphone could pick up the sound. The format differences proved difficult for some actors, so many studios were in search of fresh talent to fill their ranks. Thelma Todd managed to not only transition over to the talkies, but she excelled in her new role. This became a chance for her to show the world her comedic skill, which, it turns out, was excellent.

The famous Hal Roach, the man responsible for Laurel and Hardy, was seeking new talent for MGM and he came across Thelma. Over the span of her career she would work with now legendary comedy greats like Laurel and Hardy and the Marx Brothers. Her catalogue of films includes approximately 120 movies during the span of her nine-year career. She was such a huge hit that Roach would eventually eye her to be the first big female comedic star. In an effort to produce a female version of Laurel and Hardy he paired Thelma with actress ZaSu Pitts. A series of 'shorts' featuring Thelma ran to almost forty. It wouldn't be just comedy roles for Thelma, however. She was also an adept dramatic actor, starring opposite Sam Spade in the 1931 classic, *The Maltese Falcon.*

Her Personal Life

In 1932 Thelma married a Hollywood agent named Pat DiCicco. The two didn't last long, however, and divorced in 1934. DiCicco, who had a number of underworld connections, is said to have been physically abusive to Thelma.

In 1930 Todd took up with a married film director named Roland West. West directed several films, but his most noteworthy film may be his adaptation of the Broadway hit *The Bat*, in 1926. *The Bat* is said to be one of the inspirations for one of the most famous comic book heroes of all time: Batman.

Because West was married, he and Todd couldn't live together, but the two had apartments side by side and carried on without much regard for what anyone thought. It is said that West was rather controlling and jealous when it came to Todd. Despite being involved with West, Todd still carried on affairs with other men and the two had a difficult time keeping the peace.

Thelma struggled with the pressures of performing on the big screen and is said to have taken massive amounts of questionable diet pills to maintain her figure. It wasn't simply her own desire to remain attractive to the audiences, but her studio contract is said to include a 'potato clause' stipulation that she must maintain a certain weight range. If she gained five pounds or more she could be fired. This kept Thelma maintaining a dangerous balance of diet pills, drinking, and possibly harder drugs, although there is no confirmation of that.

A good number of actors in her era were satisfied with their lot, but Thelma was always looking for more. She would open her own successful restaurant in the summer of 1934, Thelma Todd's Sidewalk Café. It was opened on land owned by Roland West. The building still stands at 17575 Pacific Coast Highway in the Pacific Palisades area of Los Angeles, California. The venture was a joint one with West, his wife and Thelma all being part owners. The café became a destination for curious tourists and a good number of famous celebrities of the era. It would be in a garage near this elegant restaurant that her lifeless body would later be found.

The Death of a Beauty

There are a number of different theories about the evening that Thelma Todd died. She was only 29 years old when her lifeless body was found on the morning of 16 December 1935. Thelma was discovered by her maid, Mae Whitehead, who had gone to the garage of Roland West to fetch his car for him on Monday morning. She had died of carbon monoxide poisoning.

When the police investigated, they found Thelma cloaked in a lavish mauve and silver evening gown and expensive mink coat, fully adorned in jewels and with her hair done. The last time that Thelma had been seen, she was out for a night on the town at the Trocadero club. The hip night club had just opened the year before and was already a destination for the 'who's who' of Hollywood elite. She left the club and is said to have arrived home at a very late hour.

One theory is that she arrived home in the early hours of the morning, around 2.00 am, and since Roland had not gone to the party, he had wanted Thelma home by midnight. The two may have quarrelled, Thelma tried to leave, but Roland locked her in the garage. This theory has been put forth, but would only make sense if she were so thoroughly intoxicated that she had lost her wits. Otherwise, she could have simply turned off the ignition to the car and survived the night. The coroner's report did indicate that her blood alcohol level was 0.13 per cent. In order to give that number context, in the United States, if a person's blood alcohol level is above 0.08 per cent they are considered a drunk driver. It would be possible that she passed out in the car before being able to leave the premises.

Another theory is that her death was thanks to some troubles that Thelma had found with organised crime. Her maid indicated that Thelma was involved with the mob through a man named Lucky Luciano. Luciano ran a New York mob family. Lucky Luciano was introduced to Thelma by Pat DiCicco. She was attracted to danger and the idea of spending time with a mobster certainly didn't turn her away. Organised crime had set their sights out west, where the money was, and while the infamous mobster Al Capone asserted his control over the movie studios, Luciano would control gambling, drugs and prostitution. Thelma had a posh nightclub, the perfect place to try and drain money from the deep pockets of Hollywood's elite. Thelma agreed to have dinner with Lucky at the Brown Derby restaurant in Hollywood. During their evening together he tried to pressure her into allowing him to place a gambling casino in her café, but she would have none of it. The two are said to have been involved for a time, but that again ended in violence. Luciano was hoping to worm his way into Capone's territory by tricking those involved with the studios into amassing huge gambling debts through a trusted source like Thelma Todd. Thelma definitely felt that she had reason to be concerned, she had made an appointment to see the District Attorney to discuss a serious matter, but didn't live to make the appointment.

There are a few curious notes about her death that make it suspicious, such as partially digested peas and carrots in her stomach during the autopsy. Todd hadn't eaten that night at the Trocadero. Also, Roland West would never work in Hollywood again after Thelma's death. There is no solid or particularly compelling evidence that foul play was present, other than the odd conspiracy theory. It is said that Roland West provided a deathbed confession to the murder to his friend Chester Morris, but that is all simply conjecture without evidence.

Thelma could have gone to the garage to sleep off her night, having arrived home at a very late hour. She also had an existing heart condition and a penchant for fainting. In the end, the police decided that it was an accidental death by carbon monoxide poisoning. The true cause of her death will likely remain a mystery.

Legacy

Thelma is remembered as Hollywood's first great female comedian, although she is far from the only one. Todd was one of the few women to make the transition from silent films to talkies with a great level of success. Her tragically short career has been memorialised with a star on the Hollywood Walk of Fame at 6262 Hollywood Boulevard.

Chapter Three

Jean Harlow

Jean Harlow was the original Hollywood platinum-blonde sex goddess. She was the epitome of confidence, lust and seduction and when you couple that with a moderate acting talent, you have one hell of a star. She was Hollywood's original 'Blonde Bombshell', but her light would only shine brightly for a short time. Harlow's career would only span a decade, but during that time she would grace the screen for a total of thirty-six films. Her lasting legacy, however, would remain tainted by the direction her life took off the screen.

Early Life

Harlean Harlow Carpenter had a tragic childhood, rife with trauma and abuse. She was born in Kansas City, Missouri on Friday 3 March 1911. The child of Montclair, a dentist, and Jean, she grew up in a toxic environment that was anything but a loving family. Her mother and father had an arranged marriage and one that her mother greatly resented. Her mother, known as Mama Jean, held onto her dreams of becoming an actress and soon divorced Harlow's father and moved her daughter out to Hollywood. Unable to see her father, Harlow became isolated from the life she had previously known. Mama Jean was unsuccessful in her venture into fame and fortune, but she did find herself a new husband out west.

Childhood trauma

Despite the horrors to which the young Jean was exposed by her mother, she remained loyal to her. Mama Jean continued to have a stranglehold of influence over her daughter until the day she died, leaving Jean to make a series of poor decisions that would leave her life legacy a tragic tale.

Harlean began attending the Ferry Hall School in Illinois to study acting when she was just 15 years old. The venture was at the insistence of her overbearing mother, who wanted to live vicariously through her beautiful young daughter. Harlean was ill off and on for much of her youth, including a bout of Scarlet fever when she was just 15.

Harlean took the first chance she had to get out of her situation and, aged 16, found herself a suitor in Charles Fremont McGrew, a handsome 23-year-old heir to a huge family fortune. They married and fled across the country to the comfort and lavish living of Beverly Hills. Harlow was interested in becoming a wife and mother, but just a year after their marriage Charles inherited the full extent of his wealth. The couple was soon distracted from their goals, focusing instead on enjoying the spoils of the privileged elite. Harlean was suddenly a socialite and didn't need to worry herself with work or the troubles of daily life. Instead, the couple would engage in heavy bouts of drinking and partying with their friends. The young marriage would be short-lived, with the two divorcing in 1929.

Career

It was while she was living in Beverly Hills, married to McGrew that Harlean began to seek work as an extra in motion pictures. Always seeking her mother's approval, she kept making efforts to make it big, despite the disapproval of her then husband, leading to the dissolution of their union. She would get her first major film role in the 1927 *Why is a Plumber?* Harlean achieved rapid success in the pictures, starring in fifteen films between 1927 and 1929 – a journey that Mama Jean struggled with. Harlean was honing her craft and her career was gaining momentum, but she needed something to take her to the next level. In 1930 she caught the eye of the legendary Howard Hughes and it was this association that would solidify her as a legendary Hollywood sex symbol. Hughes was in the middle of making his ambitious air epic, *Hell's Angels*. Originally conceived of as a silent film, the movie began filming in 1927. Hughes was notoriously difficult to deal with and wouldn't accept anything but perfection from the cast or crew. During the filming, the emergence of sound in motion pictures caused Hughes to modify the direction of his film to become a 'talkie'. Unfortunately, his lead female, Greta Nissen, had a heavy Norwegian accent, so he had to part ways with her. Hughes recast the role of Helen, calling upon the sultry new blood of Jean Harlow to fill the role.

Howard Hughes was a fantastic businessman and, realising what he had stumbled upon, he signed Jean Harlow to a contract for $100 a week before he put in her *Hell's Angels*. Once the film was released, she quickly became a hot property and was in demand. A few years in, Hughes began to loan Jean out to other studios, like MGM, for a fee of $5,000 per week, when he had raised her wage to only $250.

Jean Harlow would be labelled as nothing more than a pretty face by many critics, but she wasn't one to rest on the laurels of her good looks. Jean strove to improve her acting and worked hard to improve in each film. Her performance in *Wife vs. Secretary* and *Libeled Lady* in particular show how she was striving to excel in her craft. Her final film role came in 1937 where she would play the character Carol Clayton in *Saratoga*, alongside the dashing Clark Gable. It was during the filming of this movie that she first became gravely ill.

Marriage to Paul Bern

While working for MGM Jean met a studio lieutenant by the name of Paul Bern. He became infatuated with her immediately and pushed for her to be cast in the film *Red Headed Woman*. The head of MGM was hesitant, but Burn insisted. The lead would make her a huge star, it was a role that all the leading women of Hollywood were vying for. Harlow dyed her platinum-blonde hair red, and history was made. She became a bit typecast after the film, which worked out well for her; on screen, she played the strong, sexy and confident woman. The act of shedding her signature platinum-blonde look was a bold one for Harlow; she had invented the image of platinum-blonde bombshell on the big screen. Her hairdresser, Alfred Pagano, helped her to bleach her hair. This is a move that hadn't been done by any big screen actresses at that point and it made a huge impression on audiences.

Despite Paul Bern being twice Harlow's age, in the summer of 1932 they were married. Their relationship was unique. According to Marcella Rabwin, legendary producer David O. Selznick's personal assistant, the couple never consummated their relationship. She insists that Bern was impotent and unable to perform. When Marcella questioned Harlow about this, Jean laughed her off, saying that she didn't care about his body, it was his mind that she loved. She thought he was brilliant and they would discuss books and opinions. It wasn't long, however, before tragedy would strike this ill-fated relationship.

About two months into their marriage, on 4 September 1932, the couple were expected to show at Mama Jean's house for dinner. Jean showed up alone, because the couple had fought earlier in the evening. The events are still unclear, but one things is for certain – this is one of Hollywood's most enduring murder mysteries. While Harlow was away at her mother's home, Paul Bern stood nude in front of his dressing room mirror, put a .38 calibre gun to his head and pulled the trigger.

Paul had a dark secret: he was a bigamist. He was married to a woman named Dorothy Millette from New York. The two had lived together so long that they had a common-law marriage. Dorothy apparently had showed up at the couple's home and this led to the fight between Paul and Jean; Jean had been unaware of this other wife.

There is some conspiracy conjecture that maybe Dorothy put the gun to Paul's head that night. No one would be able to question Dorothy, as fate would have it. She fled the scene and took a steamboat to Sacramento. She would never finish her voyage; her body was found a week later, floating in the Sacramento River.

It was time for the studio to swoop in and start damage control. The body was found by their butler. One of the MGM studio heads and Paul Selznick showed up at the house and found a suicide note left by Paul. The note read as follows:

> Dearest Dear, Unfortunately this is the only way to make good the frightful wrong I have done you and wipe out my frightful abject humiliation. l love you. Paul.
>
> P.S. You understand that last night was only a comedy.

There was a concern about preserving the studio's reputation and their star, Harlow. The note was left, so that there was no doubt that he had taken his own life.

Harlow had been dealt a duo of crushing blows. Her husband was a bigamist with a secret past, and now he was gone forever. In a move that can only be defined as absolutely character defining, Jean placed a call to Sacramento and paid to have Dorothy buried in a nice spot in the cemetery there. Harlow even purchased a headstone for her with the name 'Dorothy Millette Bern' engraved on it. Three days after the death of Paul, Jean went back to work.

Jean's next love interest was cameraman Paul Rossen. This third marriage would get her through her grief, but it lasted only seven short months. Jean was a single woman again by the beginning of 1933.

Her Death and Legacy

In 1935, Harlow and fellow MGM actor William Powell found each other on the set of the film *Reckless*. The two took up together, but sadly she wouldn't live long enough for them to marry.

Jean Harlow's flame would die out at an extremely young age. Her light was extinguished, many said, as a result of her mother's association with Christian Science and her own distasteful desire to enjoy the spotlight that her daughter couldn't seem to avoid. Harlow was said to have died as a direct result of her mother's inability to allow her access to appropriate medical care. The beliefs of the Christian Science religion will often include a denial of care by a medical professional. Jean became ill, unable to care for herself, and her mother stepped into the spotlight as the mother of the ill actress, allowing her daughter to die. This would certainly have been the story, but alas there was no hope for Jean either way.

Harlow was working with Clark Gable on the set of *Saratoga* when her health began to worsen. She had been looking pale and sickly for a while, causing many to question how she was feeling. One day she simply could not move on her own and could not work. Harlow begged co-star and friend Clark Gable to return her to her dressing room.

Powell came to visit Jean at her home. He called his own doctor and had her admitted to hospital in the hope she could be treated, but there was no saving her. The doctors thought they had Jean's condition under control, but she slipped into a coma and died soon thereafter with Powell and Mama Jean by her side, a mere eight days after having to leave the set of *Saratoga*,.

Jean Harlow died on 7 June 1937. In the end Jean succumbed to a cerebral oedema. Her brain had accumulated too much fluid, causing it to swell. She also suffered from uraemia, which indicated a serious malfunction in her kidneys and bladder. The sad reality is that there were no medical provisions that could have saved her back then. Jean's fate was sealed, no matter the path taken. She had suffered renal failure and the first kidney transplant surgeries wouldn't be performed until two decades after her death.

She was laid to rest on 9 June 1937. The funeral at Forest Lawn Cemetery was a lavish event. Her lover, William Powell, was an absolute shambles. His reaction was so heart wrenching, that it was reported in newspaper headlines. One such headline, in the San Jose News, read 'WM. Powell Sobs At Harlow Funeral'. It wasn't only Powell who openly wept at the funeral, but screen legend Clark Gable as well. The two had become close friends while working together on multiple projects.

Jean's mother arranged for a Christian Science funeral, which was attended by 200 of Jean's friends. It was a grim, but brief affair, lasting only twenty-one minutes. There were thousands of fans outside the iron gates of the cemetery, pressing and pushing to get a view of the proceedings. Powell purchased spots at the cemetery for Jean, himself and Mama Jean. She has not a grave, but a full crypt, complete with an inscription of her name and the phrase 'Our Baby'.

Saratoga was still released, with another actress standing in for Harlow in the scenes that she was unable to complete.

Harlow's legacy includes a star on the Hollywood Walk of Fame. It can be found on the south side of the 6900 block of Hollywood Boulevard.

Chapter Four

Charlie Chaplin

Summary

He is perhaps the most famous face to come out of the silent film era, but Charlie Chaplin wasn't the fun-loving and fancy-free character that he portrayed on screen in films such as *The Tramp*. A complicated and tortured artist, he was haunted by the ghosts of his past, a mother who fell into madness and an absentee father. He lived in poverty as a child and that helped to instil an intense work ethic in him that would drive him to be one of the most successful and beloved film stars of all time. His work has inspired generations of actors, directors and writers. His legacy is one of varied success. For example, he inspired cartoon characters, like the iconic Walt Disney mascot Mickey Mouse and in the same career would challenge the authority and tyranny of Adolf Hitler (and the United States government) with his satire film, *The Great Dictator*.

He was a man obsessed with his own comedic vision, often too busy for anything or anyone else in his life. He also had a taste for very young women, sometimes too young.

> I always like walking in the rain, so no one can see me crying.
>
> Charlie Chaplin

Early Life

Charles Spencer Chaplin was born in London on 16 April 1889. His mother, Hannah, was a struggling stage actress who would split with his father, Charles Chaplin Sr, just two years after little Charlie was born. His young life was filled with poverty and uncertainty, as his mother tried to get by dressmaking and nursing. The family would be forced into the cruel workhouses, but his mother sent Charlie and his brothers away to a district school for paupers before they had to go in. She would eventually be committed to an asylum, due to her madness from syphilis and malnutrition. The workhouses were no place for a healthy person, but once she was separated from her children and she was forced into the institution, her mind couldn't handle the strain. Charlie went to live with the father who had been absent from his life, both physically and financially. Two years later his father died and Charlie went back to live with his mother, who was experiencing a period of remission. The trauma of his life drove Charlie to express himself on the stage and he had quit school completely by the age of 13 to focus on his comedic act.

> Movies are a fad. Audiences really want to see live actors on a stage.
>
> Charlie Chaplin

Career Overview

Charlie's mother would relapse and soon Charlie was on the stage full-time touring to support himself, along with his brother. He was 24 by the time he decided to head to America and work in the burgeoning motion picture industry. His first job was with Keystone Studios. The head of the studio at the time, Mack Sennett, thought he looked too young to be in a Keystone film, but Charlie would win him over, just as he would the rest of America. He was already directing his first movies by the next year. During this time he began to develop his signature look for his character, *The Tramp*. He worked for Keystone for just one year, because when he asked for a raise at the end of 1914, Sennett thought he was asking for too much. Fortunately, by that point Chaplin had proven himself to be quite the asset, so the Essanay Film Manufacturing Company would snatch him up, offering him a huge signing bonus and a good contract.

Chaplin was so famous that by 1915 that there was 'Tramp' themed merchandise flooding stores and he was able to demand a salary that would make him a millionaire. Chaplin stood at a below average height of just 5ft 5in, but he attained the status of one of the most famous men in the world by the time he was 26 years old. The public was so infatuated with Chaplin that the terms 'Chaplinitis' and 'Chaplinoia' were coined to describe it. When he signed with the Mutual Film Corporation in 1916 he was one of the highest paid people in the entire world. In that same year that Chaplin would open his own studio and produce classic films such as *The Immigrant*, *The Vagabond* and *Easy Street*.

It has been said that Chaplin viewed Leni Riefenstahl's infamous pro-Nazi propaganda film *Triumph of the Will* at the New York Museum of Modern Art. Chaplin saw the absurdity in the pageantry and over-the-top aggression by the fanatical fascist Adolf Hitler. Chaplin was no fan of the Nazis and they weren't particularly fond of him either. He had visited Berlin in 1931 and was mobbed by adoring fans; not ones to share control and influence, it was a scene that didn't sit well with the Nazi Party. In a book of 1934 which took aim at famous Jews, the Nazis described Chaplin as 'a disgusting Jewish acrobat'. Chaplin wasn't actually Jewish, but it was the easiest way for the Nazis to villainise someone they didn't like. Chaplin was rapidly anti-fascist, and although he wasn't an official member of any socialist or communist political parties, as once asserted by the United States government, he did support the idea. He made his feelings clear in a 1942 interview with *The Daily Worker*, 'They say Communism may spread out all over the world. And I say – so what? I am not a Communist, but I am proud to say that I feel pretty pro-Communist.' The ideals of Communism are in direct political and social contrast with those of National Socialism, which by default made Chaplin a direct opponent of the Third Reich.

> I have always regretted not having been his partner in a longer film than these one-reelers we made so rapidly. He is a complete comic genius, undoubtedly the only one of our time and he will be the only one who will be still talked about a century from now.
>
> Fatty Arbuckle on Charlie Chaplin

Scandal and Legacy

Chaplin had a complicated relationship with women. He was quoted in a 1926 *Vanity Fair* article, titled 'Yessir, That's My Baby! – Wherein Several Experts Define the Perfect Female'. He gave his top ten list of traits that define his perfect woman, including 'I am not exactly in love with her, but she is entirely in love with me'. Chaplin was widely regarded as a sexist and though that wasn't uncommon during that era, it certainly was a glaring character flaw.

Charlie Chaplin began to have relationships with beautiful, and often young and aspiring, actresses. He started up with his 19-year-old co-star Edna Purviance. Edna would appear in thirty-three Chaplin films over the years, including classics such as *The Kid* and *The Tramp*. Charlie and Edna were an item for a good long while, but it's said that she eventually lost interest in their relationship due to Charlie's often distant attitude. Chaplin was well known to have been obsessed with his work and would go for days or weeks all but ignoring his girlfriend. Edna eventually moved on and would marry airline pilot John Squire and the two lived happily until the time of his death. Chaplin would have no troubles in moving on past Edna through, reportedly, a slew of other actresses.

He would focus most of his romantic endeavours on teenagers and women who were far too young for him. In certain cases the women weren't even legally of age, making him a statutory rapist in the state of California. That was the case with the girl he had met first when she was only 6 years old. Lita Grey was a young actress who had roles in a few of

Chaplin's features, including the *The Kid* when she was 12. It was only a few years later, during the 1924 filming of *The Gold Rush*, that her pregnancy by Chaplin was revealed at the young and quite illegal age of 15. Chaplin had assured her and their friends that he would of course marry her if she were to be found in the family way, but instead of this he pressured her into an abortion and offered to pay her off instead of wedding her. Chaplin clearly had no interest in starting a family. Grey herself detailed an instance where one of her family members literally took a shotgun off of the wall and coerced Charlie into a wedding. The two would remain married for two short years, before one of the ugliest and most prolonged divorces in Hollywood at the time.

The divorce decree between Chaplin and Lita became public when it was discovered in 2015 in the vaults of an abandoned bank in Los Angeles, California. The documents were over fifty pages long and detailed Lita's account of the cruel treatment she received at the hands of Charlie.

The documents entail a Chaplin who forced his wife to perform 'revolting degrading and offensive' acts that were illegal at the time in California. The various sodomy laws in California at the time were commonly referred to as a 'Victorian Morality Period'. The types of sexual acts that Chaplin forced Lita into weren't detailed in the documents, but we do know they included things like homosexuality, anal sex and oral sex. The teenage Lita detailed an incident where Chaplin forced her into a threesome with a woman.

> Plaintiff alleges that ever since the date of said marriage, defendant has treated plaintiff in a cruel

and inhuman manner, and has wrongfully inflicted upon her great and grievous mental suffering and anguish.

Some excerpts of the divorce decree outright accuse Chaplin of trying to pressure Lita into having an abortion, which was a highly illegal, unregulated and dangerous procedure at that time:

> ...during the month of May, 1924, plaintiff and defendant became engaged to be married; that as a result of said seduction, plaintiff became and was pregnant with child at the time of said marriage; that upon the discovery by defendant of said delicate condition of plaintiff, defendant delayed the consummation of said promise of marriage for so long a time in an effort to induce plaintiff to prevent the birth of said child by submitting herself to a criminal operation...

When Lita objected to the 'revolting' and 'degrading' acts being forced upon her by her husband, he is said to have shouted, 'All married people do those kind of things. You are my wife and you have to do what I want you to do.' The picture painted by Lita has to be taken subjectively, as a soon-to-be ex-wife probably isn't the most objective source; somewhere between Lita and Charlie's stories, however, lies the truth, and that truth undoubtedly includes at least a portion of these events.

The case of Joan Barry

The strange and salacious case of yet another trial in the life of Charlie Chaplin. This time he was accused of committing white slavery. The year was 1944 and the world was in a state of disarray. America was in the throws of the Second World War and everyone was busy with the war effort. The citizens were all chipping-in and working hard to support the troops overseas. There was a large part of the population that went about life as usual and one thing that didn't cease was scandal. Just over one year before the war came to an end, Charlie Chaplin found himself in court once more. This time the 52-year-old screen legend faced a very serious set of charges brought about by his past relationship with actress Joan Barry.

Chaplin was brought-up on charges related to the Mann Act of 1901. The law was proposed by congressman James Robert Mann of Illinois and was pitched as a way to minimise what was purported to be a human-trafficking epidemic. Although, there were those who would minimise that idea, chalking it up to fear-mongering. The law ended up being used more as a method to prosecute men for having sex with underage girls. Unsavoury men of the era had figured out that each state had a differing age of consent, so if they found a young girl they wanted to have sex with, they simply had to take her past the state line. The new law made this method obsolete, because it was now a felony to transport 'any woman or girl for the purpose of prostitution or debauchery, or for any other immoral purpose'. This also provided a way for the authorities to go after Charlie Chaplin in the case of one of his many underage girls.

Chaplin was married to his third wife in 1941, the same year he would meet the young up-and-coming actress Joan Barry. He would cast her for a film titled *Shadows and Substance*, and change the trajectory of his life forever. The two became embroiled in a romantic affair very shortly after meeting, not an uncommon set of events in Chaplin's life – he was always searching for a new muse. What made this situation different was a fateful day in 1942 when Chaplin called for Barry to join him by train in New York City. Chaplin purchased a ticket for her and brought her across the country, crossing several state lines, for the purpose of engaging in sexual acts, which was strictly prohibited by the Mann Act. Although the main consideration for the Act was to prohibit prostitution, it also included any activity that was considered to be immoral. Chaplin was brought up on charges that he 'feloniously transported and caused to be transported Joan Barry from Los Angeles to the city of New York'. Although Barry wasn't under age, she was Chaplin's mistress.

Unfortunately for Barry she wasn't fourth-wife material, but rather just a fling for Chaplin. The two quarrelled shortly after this interlude and their affair was over. This led to further accusations against Chaplin and some members of the local police department. Barry imagined that there was a criminal conspiracy to kick her out of Los Angeles after she was charged with vagrancy. All accounts state that she was in a state of instability. She went as far as to break into Chaplin's house and brandish a weapon after their breakup. When the police questioned her she told them that she had no home and no money, leading to the vagrancy charges. It is entirely possible that Chaplin did conspire to have her booted out of town, since she had become a safety concern and a potential danger to herself and others.

Joan gave birth to a baby girl in October of 1943, claiming that the father was indeed Charlie Chaplin. She took him to court over the Mann Act violation and a separate civil suit for paternity of her daughter, along with charges of violating her constitutional rights.

The trial took an important turn when the defence brought forward two prominent men, one a writer and one an oil tycoon, both of whom confirmed they were seeing her 'intimately' at the same time as she was with Chaplin. One of the main charges involved the accusation that Chaplin paid for Barry to come to New York and stay there, but if the defence could prove that Chaplin had not in fact paid for the trip, he would be completely innocent. That is exactly what they managed to do. A Tulsa-based lawyer named Claude H. Rosenstein came forward and testified that he handled the payments to Barry for the trip, and had proof. He also verified that he was not working for Chaplin, but did not state on whose behalf he was working.

On 4 April 1944 the jury, consisting of five men and seven women, cleared Chaplin on both counts of violating the Mann Act. Their reasoning was that 'The fact that a journey from one State to another is followed by illicit intercourse, where the journey was not for that purpose, but wholly for other reasons cannot be regarded as a violation of the so-called Mann Act.' The jury felt that the government did not present sufficient evidence as to Chaplin's intent.

The issue of paternity should have been open-and-shut after Chaplin passed blood tests by three separate physicians proving he was not the father. Unfortunately for Chaplin, in California at the time blood tests were inadmissible in court. Barry had agreed to drop the suit if the blood tests found that Chaplin was not the father, but decided to proceed anyway. The courts found that the agreement to drop the suit wasn't binding and the trial proceeded later that year.

Chaplin married his fourth and final wife, Oona O'Neill, just two week after the paternity charges were filed by Barry in 1943. Oona had just turned 18, giving a thirty-six year age gap between the two.

Red Scare Scandal and Banishment from America

The aftermath of the Second World War left one-time allies Russia and the United States in the throes of a Cold War. The two would turn on each other almost immediately, ushering in decade upon decade of spy games, espionage, threats and secrets. Prior to the war there had been advocates and talk of Communism in America, and the idea wasn't altogether unpopular.

The Red Scare was a government-sponsored witch hunt that found the United States government putting people on a mock trial to verify their supposed loyalty to the country. Anyone suspected of being a Communist or Socialist was subject to government scrutiny. It wasn't the first time that a 'Red Scare' had washed across America. The Bolshevik Revolution sent waves of terror across the ocean and the idea of a citizen revolt became a very real possibility. What followed was a fear of European immigrants bringing their revolutionary attitudes over to America and overthrowing the country in the name of their new Communist agenda. This fear-mongering was often spread by unscrupulous newspapers, looking to boost sales.

The Communist witch hunts began with government employees, testing their dedication to America and the democracy that was held so dear. Anti-Communist propaganda began to emerge and the target of much of the scrutiny was, what is still to this day considered by many, the 'Hollywood Elite'. In 1950 this idea went from talk to action when a right-wing publication, *Counterattack*, produced a propaganda pamphlet titled *Red Channels*. This inflammatory document listed 151 different writers, directors, actors and producers that supposedly held highly liberal beliefs that were a danger to America. A few of these accused crimes come across as laughable today, and include a belief and support of ideas like 'peace', 'civil rights' and 'academic freedom'. The introduction of the pamphlet speaks volumes as to the tone:

> No cause which seems calculated to arouse support among people in show business is ignored: the overthrow of the Franco dictatorship, the fight against anti-Semitism and Jimcrow, civil rights, world peace, the outlawing of the H-Bomb, are all used. Around such pretended objectives, the hard core of Party organisers gather a swarm of 'reliables' and well-intentioned 'liberals,' to exploit their names and their energies.

What should have been a harmless bit of propaganda instead began to serve as a blacklist that would keep these individuals from obtaining work in many areas of their industry.

The Hollywood Ten

There were only ten members of the supposed Hollywood Elite that actually appeared in front of the House Un-American Activities Committee in the autumn of 1947. This diverse group of directors, producers and writers were called upon more because of their liberal mindset than any actual political affiliations. The group stood on principle and refused to answer the committee questions, which found them in contempt of Congress. They were all sentenced to prison time, ranging from six months to a year as a reprisal for their stance. The red blacklist wouldn't last long and by the 1960s it had all but been admonished and disavowed.

In the midst of McCarthyism there were other high-profile celebrities that would be heavily associated with the anti-Communist agenda. The list would include Helen Keller, Lucille Ball, Orson Welles, composer Leonard Bernstein and Charlie Chaplin. Chaplin, however, had become a target of the FBI decades earlier when he caught the attention of J. Edgar Hoover. Chaplin and Hoover had a social interaction that had gone poorly and Hoover was convinced that Chaplin, as an immigrant who spoke out and criticised the government, was suspect and would do his best to drum-up any dirt on the superstar. It wasn't until the McCarthy-era Red Scare that he would finally be able to take real action against Chaplin.

In 1952 Charlie Chaplin would leave American soil onboard the *Queen Elizabeth* to attend the premiere of his film *Limelight* in London. He was constantly embroiled in the anti-Communist controversy in America and commented on his position while at a press conference for the film. Chaplin insisted that he was simply someone who 'wants nothing more for humanity than a roof over every man's head'.

This was J. Edgar Hoover's chance to be rid of the man that he considered a 'one of Hollywood's parlor Bolsheviks'. The news came to Chaplin that the FBI was denying his return visa to the United States, citing him as a security risk. He was kept out with an accusation of violating the White Slave Traffic Act and for a violation of civil liberties. Hoover was so convinced that Chaplin was up to no good that he reached out to MI5 and asked them to keep tabs on him. The MI5 files that would later become declassified found no cause to think of Chaplin as any type of security threat.

Chaplin could have fought the decision, but it is generally accepted that he was so disgusted by the current state of his adopted country that he simply gave in and instead moved to Switzerland, far away from the scrutiny of the American public. He famously stated that he wouldn't return to America, even if Jesus Christ himself were president.

Ironically, the next year an internal FBI memo stated that there was insufficient evidence to back-up the claim and that they would not be able to hold-up the denial of entry. This had been the final straw for Chaplin, who would remain banished to Switzerland for decades, until his eventual return in 1972 to receive a well deserved honorary Academy

Award. It was revealed in 1986 by Chaplin biographer David Robinson that the FBI, flawed and sloppy as their research proved to be, maintained an interest in Chaplin well after his death in 1977.

Legacy

The life of Charlie Chaplin was certainly one with a high level of drama. His legacy was helped along by a well-received feature film in 1992 starring Robert Downey Jr as the complex and talented comedian. He was named among *Time* magazine's '100 Most Important People of the 20th Century', and has been called a 'towering figure in world culture' by the British Film Institute. There are statues of Chaplin featured in sights in London, Slovakia, Ireland, Switzerland, Italy, India, Spain and Poland. He has had a star on the Hollywood Walk of Fame since 1972. His films also continue to delight and, unlike many vintage films, continue to hold-up in quality and content.

Chapter Five

Mae West

Mae West had a career that began on the legendary stages of vaudeville and transitioned into one of the most-in-your-face, unapologetic sexual icons of her time. She stared a repressed American culture in the face with her often blunt and unabashed sexuality on the stage, a bravery that would someday bring her screaming onto the worldwide forum of the silver screen.

If you look to the past to find one star that created a blueprint for the future, it would be Mae West. Today's world of entertainment is full of women who have taken what could have been scandal and turned it into illustrious careers. Kim Kardashian, for example, managed to parlay her sex tape into superstardom. Mae West is no Kim K., but she certainly had her fair share of sex-based scandal. In fact, it was the 1925 Broadway offering titled *Sex* that would change her life forever and set her on a path to superstardom.

Early Life

Mae was born just before the turn of the century, on 17 August 1893. Mae, whose given name was Mary Jane West, was raised on the mean streets of Brooklyn, New York. Her father, John West, was a rough-and-tough boxer who was known locally for his work in the ring – primarily in violent and unsanctioned underground matches. Her mother, Matilda, was a striking immigrant from Germany who moonlighted as a fashion model. Matilda worked as a garment worker by day, but she had big dreams of becoming a star. Mae was often indulged by her mother and instead of having a childhood that was full of harsh punishments, like many children of the age, she was all too often encouraged to be difficult and full of spirit. Mae would retain the self confidence and self assurance that she gained from her relationship with her mother all through her life.

Career

Mae would get a small taste for performing when she was just 5 years old by performing at a church social. Her mother was always a strong influence on her and Mae would be exposed to the world of vaudeville from the age of 14. Matilda was enthralled with the stage and soon Mae would become involved in the process herself, performing under the stage name 'Baby Mae' for the Hal Clarendon Stock Company. Mae was a young stage performer, but she found attention and success, causing her initially sceptical father to devote his time and energy to enthusiastically supporting her burgeoning career. Her show would largely consist of her playing-up her youthful and innocent look, all the while engaging the audience in a series of double entendres and songs that oozed adult sexuality. Mae was already forming the persona that would find her international fame. Matilda became her manager, handling her training and bookings in the local entertainment industry. It was her mother's way of breaking into showbiz and being involved in the glamour of the world she so desperately craved.

Mae continued to perform, but under the stage name of 'Jane Mast'. She made her Broadway debut in 1911, albeit in a small role in a revue that would be short lived. Mae would go on to use her stage name as a nom de plume and began writing risqué plays. It would be this writing that would help to create the greatest controversy of her life – and her time.

I believe in censorship. I made a fortune out of it
Mae West

Sex

Mae West will go down in history as one of the first actresses to push the boundaries of sexuality in the public eye. Not only did she push the boundaries, she broke them whenever possible. The controversy all surrounded a Broadway production. It seems odd in today's world that a Broadway show would bring such public outcry, but when Mae West starred in *Sex*, it was a bold and confident display that the American public weren't quite ready for. Not only did West star in the show, she also wrote and produced it. This wasn't just a stunt by West or something she stumbled into, Mae quite deliberately crafted this show from top to bottom. She used her time in vaudeville as inspiration to create the most sexualised show that she could imagine at the time – and the public stood up to take notice.

The newspaper critics were unsurprisingly harsh when reviewing *Sex*. The New York papers, from the *Times* to *The New Yorker*, all gave scathing outlooks on the quality and content of the show. If the play was destined to live or die by what you might consider a 'typical' and proper Broadway audience in today's world, perhaps it would have been short-lived. Fortunately for West, however, this was the burgeoning Jazz Age and there was a progressive movement towards the openness of sex and sexuality. The reviews openly mocked the blatant sexuality and explicit nature of the play, which would actually drive curious audiences into the theatre, giving the show more longevity than any other on Broadway that year.

The ticket sales were high and there was definite interest, but the 'powers that be' were not amused. The show ran for eleven months and entertained approximately 325,000 people, but all that would change in February 1927. The New York City police eventually raided the theatre and arrested Mae West for 'corrupting the morals of the youth'. West would be levied a fine of $500 and sentenced to ten days in a workhouse, which she served on Welfare Island. The prison stint didn't hurt her career though, in fact it only made her a bigger star. She handled her incarceration with dignity and grace, arriving to serve her time in a limousine. Not surprisingly, she managed to charm the pants off of the warden and his wife. West dined with the couple and got preferential treatment, even getting an early release after eight days – for good behaviour of course. It was during this time in 'jail' that West would begin penning her future hit, *Diamond Lil*.

Diamond Lil would release in 1928 and her next play, *The Constant Sinner*, in 1931. She found reasonable success on Broadway, but the pictures soon came calling.

Film Career

Mae would find her big screen debut with the boxing film *Night after Night* in 1932. She absolutely stole the show with her high-calibre acting and dynamic presence. All her efforts on the stage had truly paid off. She would become an international sex symbol, even though she wouldn't debut on the big screen until the age of 39. It was a move that was well-calculated by West and Paramount Studios. They forked out over $5,000 to Mae for her to take part in the film. To put that in perspective, it would be a payday of over $88,000 (approximately £67,000) today. Mae would go on to be such a huge success in pictures that by 1935 she was the highest paid woman in the United States.

Change began to flow through Hollywood in 1934, however, and censorship codes were more thoroughly enforced. This would end up cutting a lot of content from Mae's screenplays and would alter whatever risqué content the public might have seen from her after that point. Mae would still go on to have a very successful film career, with highlights including *Go West, Young Man*, *The Heat's On* and *Goin' To Town*.

Mae West – Bigamist

Mae went from being a popular local solo act to teaming up with another Vaudeville song and dance talent by the name of Frank Wallace. Matilda introduced the two with a vision for Mae's future. The duo began to practice and Matilda booked them on a nationwide burlesque tour circuit. The streetwise and headstrong Mae soon found herself on the road, landlocked in the middle of America and surrounded by other stage performers. Her mother and father stayed back in Brooklyn, so this was her first real taste of independence. Never one to squander an opportunity, Mae reportedly began to sleep around with several of the other cast members, all the while spurning the advances from Wallace. Frank had a mind to make Mae as his wife, but she wasn't interested in being a 15-year-old child-bride. Instead, Mae was clearly looking to drink from the cup of life and enjoy her moments with vigour and independence. Matilda had encouraged her daughter to be a spitfire and that is exactly what she had a mind to be. That is until she was put in her place by an elder member of the tour. The story goes that Etta Wood pulled Mae aside to school her on the way she had been carrying herself on the tour, telling her that she was looking for trouble.

We know that soon after Mae finally gave in to the pleadings of Frank Wallace and the two would secretly marry on 11 April 1911 in Milwaukee, Wisconsin. The tale goes that Mae might have thought she was pregnant and this gave her someone to take responsibility for it. There's no way to know for certain what motivated Mae at the time, but we do know that their marriage wasn't a success and it was a decision that West would quickly come to regret. According to West the marriage was never consummated and she opted to keep it a secret from her family. In fact, the two would remain legally married until decades later when they were granted a divorce in 1943.

West kept her legal marriage a secret for many years and would undergo scrutiny once the secret was uncovered. Mae insisted that the two were never really a couple and didn't actually live as husband and wife. West was a Hollywood star when a filing clerk stumbled upon her marriage licence and sold her out to the press in 1935.

In 1937 a lawsuit broke the scandal wide open. Frank Wallace first attempted to sue Mae under the name of Mae Wallace in the New York court system in late 1936. He claimed that the couple lived together until 1914, when she up and left without warning or cause. Wallace was advised by the courts to sue Mae in California. Frank soon took his claims out west and, on 3 May 1937, he filed a complaint against the screen legend.

The newspapers all around the United States reported on the scandal. The claim in the public was that Mae was worth $3 million, which would be more like $53 million (approximately £40 million) today.

The legal wrangling went on until that summer, when Wallace came to court and withdrew his claim for $1,000 in monthly support. Then, Mae was granted a divorce from her cross-complaint. Wallace made a statement to the court, saying 'I never wanted to bring this suit in the first place. All I wanted to do was my work.'

This proved to be quite a scandal back in those days, but it was nothing that Mae wasn't used to. Her overt sexuality and pushing of social boundaries would become her greatest scandals and her lasting legacy. Ironically, Mae would avert what would have been the biggest piece to this salacious puzzle – she was actually a bigamist.

Mae, you see, had married again during her time away from Frank Wallace. In 1913 she met a charming and dashing accordion player named Guido Deiro. The two were both vaudeville performers and the couple married in secret sometime between 1913 and 1914. The two became a duo act and toured together. They stayed together happily until 1916 when Mae's mother saw the dangers in the marriage and how they would affect her ambitions for Mae's career. West would abandon Guido at her mother's urging. Mae would later petition the courts for a divorce on the grounds of adultery in 1920. The two didn't see each other again until 1943, when they renewed their friendship.

Legacy

Mae West became such a recognisable sex symbol during her time that the Allied Air Force used the slang term 'Mae Wests' to describe their life vests. It was impossible to mention Mae without sexuality being involved in the same breath. This isn't to impugn her acting prowess, because it was not just her presence, looks and risqué attitude, but also her fine acting that would solidify her as a silver-screen legend. Salvador Dali would incorporate her image into a painting, she graced the cover of The Beatles *Sgt. Pepper's Lonely Hearts Club Band* album, along with countless other references over the years.

She would live a full life, dying on 22 November 1980, at the age of 87. Her star on the Hollywood Walk of Fame can be found on the East side of the 1500 block of Vine Street.

Chapter Six

Errol Flynn

Errol Flynn was a larger-than-life personality, on and off the silver screen. Once called the 'most beautiful man who ever lived' by Joan Crawford, he was a dashing and debonair swashbuckler in his films and a notorious hedonist and party boy in his personal life. On the outside, he had everything one could imagine in a dashing movie star. His career is legendary, but with a vivacious sexual appetite and a Peter Pan complex there was bound to be danger on this horizon.

Early Life

Errol Leslie Thomson Flynn was born on 20 June 1909 on Hobart, the capital city of the Australian island state of Tasmania.

Flynn was a handful from the start and was expelled from school on more than one occasion. This punishment came as a result of accusations of thievery and seducing girls. Flynn had a clear love of danger and a penchant for recklessness, even as a boy.

He wasn't destined for higher education, so Errol began to work at a young age. He was just 17 when he set out on his own to make his fortunes in the world, hoping to strike gold. Fired from his first job in Sydney, he travelled between there and Papua New Guinea, working various jobs from mining to farm work. It is conjectured, although unproven, that Flynn may have worked as a 'blackbirder' for a time. The idea behind blackbirding was to trick or coerce trusting and otherwise naive natives from the pacific islands into slavery. This despicable practice was very common at the time. According to the *Errol Flynn Secret Lives* documentary, Flynn also killed a native during his time as a blackbirder, a crime to which he plead his innocence and was never held accountable for.

It was time to move on for Flynn, so he set his sights back on Australia. He used his good looks and debonair persona to worm his way into polite society. He would move on soon, however, after being accused of taking advantage of a wealthy socialite and stealing her jewels. In 1933, when Flynn was 24, he tried a new path, one that would set the trajectory for the rest of his life. He obtained a role in an Australian film titled *In the Wake of the Bounty*, a documentary feature on the mutiny aboard the HMS *Bounty*. This would set Flynn on a new path that would guide the rest of his days.

Career

Flynn took his rugged good looks and his new-found interest in acting and made his way to the British Northampton Repertory Company. He drew in crowds with his looks and charm, but this gig wouldn't last long. Flynn was said to have argued with the director's wife and thrown her down a staircase.

Flynn soon moved to London. He would find roles in a handful of British films before Hollywood came calling. He had only been acting for about a year when Warner Brothers signed him to a seven-year contract from across the pond in America in 1935. Flynn advertised himself in his resumé as a world-class boxer, which was in no way accurate. He bluffed and charmed his way into fortune and eternal fame. Flynn had finally found his calling in life and it was about to make him a household name. Unfortunately for Flynn, being an actor would also allow him to lead the self-destructive lifestyle that he was so set on pursuing.

Flynn was cast in the lead of the Warner Brothers film *Captain Blood*, a big budget swashbuckling epic. He was an absolute natural on the screen, impressing the executives at Warner Brothers with his ability to execute the fight scenes properly and with little work. The film turned out to be a huge hit for the era, making Warner Brothers a lot of money and making Flynn a star. He was an overnight success, marketed as a clean-cut idol by the studios. He played the part publicly, but it couldn't have been further from the truth.

He would continue to star in various features, until hitting his most famous role in 1938 with *The Adventures of Robin Hood*. It was the most ambitious feature that Warner Brothers had bankrolled to that point. They had lot of confidence in Flynn and it paid off, with the studio making a huge profit. Flynn would continue to work through the years of the Second World War, trying to keep his reputation as an adventurer and brave tough guy, despite claims by the public and press that he was a draft dodger.

Lifestyle

One thing that can always be said about Errol Flynn is that he was never a let down. Often, when an actor is off the screen or stage they are disappointingly vapid or dull, but not Flynn. A true hedonist through and through, Flynn would spend the majority of his career partying heavily with constant smoking, drunken binges and even narcotics abuse. An avid partygoer, he would attend the now legendary gatherings held by newspaper man William Randolph Hearst. Hearst may best be known as one of the subjects whose own decadent life was spoofed in the classic Orson Welles film, *Citizen Kane*.

The parties at Hearst Castle were well known for the over-the-top indulgence and opulence. The celebrity guest list would include everyone that was anyone in Hollywood at the time. The lavishly decorated estate featured elements from various points in European history. The castle was somewhat of a retreat for the wealthy and famous friends of Hearst. It wouldn't be out of the ordinary to find the likes of Cary Grant, Clark Gable or Greta Garbo in attendance, rubbing elbows with Charlie Chaplin and the great Errol Flynn. The parties were often thematic, inviting the attendees to let loose and dress up as their favourite historical character, part of the circus, or as a childlike version of themselves for the 'kid party'. The giant rooms would be filled with tables of partygoers all drinking and relishing in the privilege of their station, an oasis from the rest of the world. Flynn would often attend these parties and it is said that he was actually thrown out of one for being excessively drunk.

Flynn managed to marry a few times, despite his partying lifestyle. His first wife, Lili Damita, stayed with him for seven years. Married in 1935, the couple would go on to have a son named Sean. The relationship between Lili and Errol was full of fire and violence. Lili was known for being extremely jealous. Unfortunately for her and Errol, women came far too easily for the handsome actor and he wasn't interested in saying 'no'. Their fights would often consist of her lashing out at him physically and throwing things.

When Flynn and Lili divorced he stayed single for a time, moving in with fellow bachelor David Niven in his seaside home. The two had a merry ol' time courting ladies and partying it up. This would last less than a year, as Flynn would soon find wife number two.

In 1943 Flynn married Nora Eddington, an attractive socialite who managed to feature in minor roles in several films; the marriage lasted six years and they had two daughters, Deidre and Rory. The origins of their relationship will be explained later in this chapter. Flynn started experimenting with drugs during their relationship; he wanted to try everything, reportedly indulging in marijuana, cocaine and heroin. His hedonism was so extensive that he felt he could overcome and dominate anything and that it wouldn't hurt him. Flynn soon settled on an addiction to morphine and it destroyed his marriage. He always believed he could stop, but his delusion overcame him. Nora would later claim that Flynn attacked her physically while on drugs and she was pregnant.

In 1950, Flynn settled down yet again, this time with Patrice Wymore. Patrice was an aspiring actress who enjoyed roles opposite famous, albeit far more successful names, like Doris Day and Kirk Douglas. The couple had one daughter, named Arnella Roma. This would prove to be Flynn's most lasting relationship, as they were together for nine years, until the time of his death.

> I intend to live the first half of my life. I don't care about the rest.
>> Errol Flynn from *My Wicked, Wicked Ways*

Sexual Proclivity

Errol Flynn was a ladies man in every sense of the phrase. He claimed to have engaged in over 12,000 sexual conquests in his day, a number that could be overblown, but there is no way of knowing for certain. Flynn lost his virginity when he was 12 and rumours persisted about the size of his phallus. The word was that it was rather large, a rumour that he did his best to encourage. The less than titillating reality was that Errol was of perfectly average size.

Flynn's home was yet another example of his voracious sexual appetites. Years after his death it was revealed that his home had a variety of two-way mirrors and secret peep holes, so that Flynn could spy on his house guests and indulge his voyeuristic side.

He never had to learn politeness or restraint when it came to his interactions with women. Flynn was able to indulge in his fantasies and often said he had no limits with sex. He would always try to go as far as a woman would let him, always pushing their boundaries.

> I like my whiskey old and my women young.
>> Errol Flynn

Statutory Rape Trial

Flynn had a long and storied history with underage girls and he seemed to purposefully gravitate there. It was only a matter of time before he would be brought up on legal charges for his crimes of seducing teenagers. He may have been debonair on screen, but his tastes in women reflect an insecure and shallow real-life persona.

Errol was at a party, not an unfamiliar setting for him. It was in September of 1942 and the arrival of a wide-eyed guest by the name of Betty Hansen. She had arrived at the home of Frederick McEvoy, a friend of Flynn's. A lot of drinking later, Flynn was said to have coerced the underage girl into sex. Actress Peggy Satterlee also accused Flynn of seducing her on his yacht, *Sirocco*.

The trial made worldwide news – it was such a story that it actually usurped coverage of the war on the front page of the newspapers. Here was this handsome, charming movie star, facing a jail term if convicted. It has been suggested that Flynn had made arrangements to flee the country if he were to be convicted. He wouldn't be going to jail.

Flynn's attorney, Jerry Giesler, took the crooked and immoral approach that is still often done today and he attacked the character of the victims. He dug into their past and tried to impugn their reputations, instead of dealing with the accusations of the crimes of which Flynn was accused. He hired investigators who learned all about the girls and dug up any dirt they could to tarnish their reputations. The cross-examination of Hansen was so severe that it left her fleeing the courtroom in tears, according to the newspapers at the time. Sexual assault, in all of its forms, is the only type of crime where the victim and their character goes on trial.

A jury comprised of nine women and three men sat on the trial, and the dashing movie star was, unsurprisingly, acquitted of all charges on 6 February 1943. The members of the jury would later equate their decision to feeling that the girls weren't completely honest. Details of their stories would differ slightly over time and that was enough to convince them not to convict. This was a man who unabashedly slept with underage girls. According to recent research, the teenage brain isn't fully developed until 25 years of age, so if a scared and bewildered 15-, or even 17-year-old, cannot remember every detail of a traumatising encounter, it wouldn't be surprising.

Incredibly, during his breaks in the trial Flynn spent his time hitting on the teenage girl that ran the cigarette stand. The legend goes that Flynn invited her home with him; she went on to become his second wife. Nora Eddington was only 18 years old when the 34-year-old actor started a romance with her. She became pregnant and to avoid scandal so soon after the trial, Flynn married her in Mexico.

In the aftermath of the trial, Flynn's fans were thrilled at the decision. He was greeted with a lot of fanfare outside the courtroom, and went on to enjoy the rest of his career.

Hansen's life, on the other hand, was ruined. Hounded by the press and looked down upon, she was never the same again. Neither she nor Peggy spoke of it for decades. Fifty years later, Hansen finally broke her silence on what happened. She had come from Nebraska to find her fame and fortune in the pictures. She says that she met Flynn at a studio party and he attacked her when she was drunk. According to Hansen there was plenty of evidence for the prosecution to work with. She was bruised and her skin was torn. Hansen says she was examined by police after the incident.

The sordid details of Flynn's personal life had been made very public, but despite this Hollywood doubled down on his 'good guy' image. This is an all but forgotten aspect of Flynn's life today and certainly isn't often mentioned. In fact, it was from this infamous trial that the term 'In Like Flynn' was coined in the vernacular.

In 1957, the 48-year-old Flynn had a sexual relationship with another impressionable 15-year-old girl, Beverly Aadland. This would later be dramatised in the feature film *The Last of Robin Hood*, starring Kevin Kline and Dakota Fanning in 2013. His drinking and drug abuse had aged Flynn considerably by his late 40s. He and Beverly Aadland met on the set of one of his films, she was 15 and looked every day of it; Flynn sent for her and she went to meet him. Beverly recounts that Flynn forced himself on her the first night they were together. She tried to stay away from him and not have contact after that night. She was terrified to tell her family for fear they would think less of her. Flynn managed to charm her, although already married. He got a vasectomy reversal and wanted to impregnate Beverly. They were going to have a New Year's Day wedding. It never happened, because he would die that autumn.

Errol Flynn: Nazi Spy?

When the Second World War began to heat-up, many of the Hollywood stars signed up for the draft. Celebrities like

Jimmy Stewart, Henry Fonda and Clark Gable. Flynn too attempted to sign up, only to be disappointed when he was rejected. He was outwardly the model of health, but the military would rate him medically 4F. This meant that he was unfit for service in the armed forces. Errol had latent pulmonary tuberculosis, spots on his lungs, a menagerie of venereal diseases and recurrent malaria from his time in New Guinea. The image of physical heroic perfection was suddenly shattered.

The studio lied and released a statement that said Flynn had a minor heart murmur. The press would speculate that he was trying to worm his way out of the war, but he was actually very keen to prove himself. Flynn even wrote to the president asking to be used as a spy for the United States. Roosevelt declined the offer.

He was forced to find excitement in other places, denied his ability to prove his masculinity in the war efforts. He would find a plethora of women to satisfy his urge, mostly girls, many of whom were under the legal age of consent, as discussed earlier in this chapter.

There was a huge movement within the Nazi party to recruit as many celebrities and well-known faces as they could prior to and during the Second World War. Not only could they use these people as well-placed propaganda pieces, but that they could also move around without notice or suspicion, giving the Nazis an upper hand when engaging in espionage.

Flynn wasn't satisfied with simply being an actor, he had a desire to become a serious writer, as well. This secret ambition caused him to publish several articles and two novels. Both claimed to be based on fact, but he found no success with them. He was regarded by the public only as a pretty face. The reality was that you can't do two things at the same time in Hollywood. Once you had found success, you were pigeon-holed. It was the first time he had encountered a difficulty in getting what he wanted out of life, so he promptly moved on to a form of writing that would more adequately suit his demeanour.

Flynn started emulating his on-screen personas and would soon dream of being a legitimate war correspondent like his hero, Ernest Hemingway. During this time in his life, Flynn became acquainted with an Austrian doctor by the name of Hermann Erben – an unabashed hedonist. He lived his life by the credo 'Do what thou wilt', which played right into the lifestyle in which Flynn felt he should be allowed to indulge.

Flynn found the trouble he was looking for during the Spanish civil war; he got a commission to write about the war and decided to take Erban along as his official photographer. Unlike Flynn, who was engaging in a fantasy adventure for the danger and romanticism, there was a more sinister reason for Erban to be there.

Erben would later admit to American authorities that he was actually there as a German spy. Hermann was a card-carrying Nazi who was thrown out of Austria for dressing like Hitler. Erben joined the Nazis in 1938 and began working as an agent for the Ehrardt Bureau of the Abwehr. He was on the radar of intelligence authorities in the United States and was even regarded as one of their most dangerous operatives when he was embedded in Mexico.

While Flynn was engrossed in his Spanish war adventures, Erben took thousands of photographs of the German expatriates fighting in the International Brigade. Hermann forwarded the photographs to the Gestapo, who would later use the information to persecute many of these people. There have been suggestions made over the past few decades that Flynn was himself a Nazi spy. Unfortunately for Flynn, he wasn't so devious as to be useful to the Nazis as an agent, but he was an easy foil for Erben to use. Dr Erben died 1985 and if Flynn had been knowingly involved in any Nazi schemes, he took that information to his grave. The reality was that Flynn wasn't interested in politics and had no sympathies to any side.

Weekend at Barrymore's

There is a legend that goes around Hollywood, perpetuated by Errol Flynn himself. The tale goes as follows: that when legendary screen actor John Barrymore died in 1942, director Raoul Walsh borrowed the body from the funeral home prior to the burial. He is said to have set the body up with a drink in hand to rib on Errol Flynn, as he returned to his home after a night of drinking. Flynn recounts these events in his autobiography and Walsh also corroborates the events in a 1973 documentary called *The Men Who Made the Movies*. A good friend of Barrymore states that this never did happen, as he and his son held a vigil at the funeral home all that night. The truth may never be known, but it certainly makes for a great tale.

Death and Legacy

Doctors employed by the film studios said that Errol Flynn had an enlarged heart and malaria way back when he was 28.

Chapter One: Evelyn Nesbit

Evelyn Nesbit. (Library of
Congress Prints and Photographs
Division, circa 1900)

Evelyn Nesbit: American Beauty.
(Author Unknown, circa 1901)

Chapter Two: Thelma Todd

The Haunted House lobby card. (First National Pictures, 1928)

Thelma Todd's sidewalk cafe. (Library of Congress)

Chapter Three: Jean Harlow

The crypt of Jean Harlow. (Arthur Dark, 2014)

Hell's Angels movie poster.

Chapter Four: Charlie Chaplin

Charlie Chaplin lobby card.

Chapter Five: Mae West

Mae West. (circa 1936)

Mae West in
her apartment
in Los Angeles.
(Allen Warren, 1973)

The Adventures of Robin Hood lobby card. (1938)

Don Juan lobby card. (1948)

Chapter Seven: Lana Turner

Above: Lana Turner in *The Three Musketeers*.

Left: Lana Turner in *Honky Tonk*. (publicity still, circa 1941)

Chapter Eight: William Desmond Taylor

The Gentleman Director: William Desmond Taylor.

Chapter Nine: Joan Crawford

Above: Outside Grauman's Chinese Theatre. (Sailko, 2010)

Left: Joan Crawford. (Library of Congress, 1927)

Mommie Dearest book cover. (MacNabb, 2018)

Chapter Ten: Barbara LaMarr

Barbara La Marr and friends. (Library of Congress, 1900)

Chapter Eleven: Mabel Normand

Mabel Normand. (*Motion Picture Magazine*, 1915)

Young Mabel Normand. (Library Of Congress, 1900)

Fatty's mug shot. (1921)

Fatty and Mabel Normand title card. (Keystone)

Chapter Thirteen: Clara Bow

Clara Bow, broadway actress. (Library of Congress, 1924)

He collapsed frequently on set, a fact that wasn't public knowledge at the time. His short life would find him riddled with many illnesses, mostly related to excessive drinking.

The last year of Flynn's life was an all-time low point for the once successful actor. His body was beaten up from years of drinking and drug abuse. His debts had also begun to get the best of him and he was forced to sell his prized possession: his yacht.

A hedonist to his last, Flynn landed in Vancouver in October 1950 with his teenage girlfriend, Beverly Aadland. When asked by reporters why he always surrounded himself with teenagers, he is said to have quipped, 'Because they f*** so good'. One fateful night, Flynn was visiting a doctor friend in Vancouver. He stopped to get a drink and began to complain about back pain and suffered his fourth and final heart attack that night. Errol Flynn was dead at the age of 50.

Flynn was laid to rest at Forest Lawn Memorial Park in Glendale, California. His tombstone is rather a humble one, considering his legacy. It says simply 'Errol Flynn June 20, 1909 – October 14, 1959' and contains the message 'In memory of our father from his loving children'.

Chapter Seven

Lana Turner

Early Life

Lana was born Julia Jean Turner on 8 February 1921 in a small mining community in Idaho. Her father, John Virgil Turner, was a miner with a bad gambling habit. The family struggled financially for years, until finally moving to San Francisco in search of a new life. Lana's mother and father would soon divorce, but that would be the least of the traumas of her young life. In 1930, when Lana was only 9 years old, her father was bludgeoned to death and robbed after winning a craps game. The loss of her father had a profound effect on Lana and many theorise that it would forever tarnish her ability to have a lasting relationship with any of the men in her life.

Career

Lana Turner was discovered at a soda fountain. Billy Wilkson, publisher of the *Hollywood Reporter*, walked to a corner cafe on a very hot day in 1937. He noticed Lana sitting there and he introduced himself to her, asking her if she'd like to be in motion pictures.

When MGM brought her into the fold, they felt that she would be a good replacement for Jean Harlow. The studio felt that she possessed a certain sex appeal that would translate well on the big screen. Turner was even pressured to adapt Harlow's signature platinum blonde hair, which she did in 1941 and maintained for the rest of her days.

Turner enjoyed regular work as the wide-eyed beauty and love interest. It was her dynamic and complex role in *The Postman Always Rings Twice* that began to set her apart. Lana was able to play the roles of femme fatale, not just a love interest. This would lead to more interesting roles in films like *Love Has Many Faces*, *Madame X* and *Peyton Place*.

Lana had a brief marriage in 1940 to fellow actor Artie Shaw. The impulsive union is barely worth mentioning, lasting only four months. Lana would later have a daughter with her second husband, Joseph Steven Crane, on 25 July 1943. Cheryl Crane was born to an almost immediately broken household, as her parents parted ways in the year of her birth. Cheryl was a Hollywood child through and through. A series of nannies and boarding school raised her as a young girl and she would be brought out for photo opportunities with her mother from time to time. The two didn't have terrible relationship, but it was certainly more formal than many.

Murder

The name John Stompanato Jr would be one that came to haunt Lana and would forever be tied to her legacy. Stompanato was a thug and a mobster. The mob was working for some time to get a grip on Hollywood and Turner was their way in through Stompanato. He was assigned to seduce and marry her, so that he could become a producer and open more doors for the mafia to tighten their grip on Hollywood.

Stompanato was well known for his association with mobster Mickey Cohen. He was so well known, in fact, that he had to use an alias to woo Turner. He began sending gifts to her on the set using an assumed name. She would eventually get tipped off about who he was and they began their tumultuous on-again, off-again romance.

The thought is that he became angry and violent with Lana once she tried to end things with him. He couldn't very well go back home and face his mob bosses empty handed. Stompanato tried his best to coerce Lana into staying with him, but it was to no avail. Lana had very little attention span when it came to her lovers. This was a woman who was married seven times, and that doesn't count boyfriends.

Stompanato beat Turner while they were in England. She was filming a movie with Sean Connery at the time. He hit and choked her, trying to suffocate her with a pillow. The incident didn't go unnoticed and Sean Connery himself is said to have threatened Stompanato over the incident. Apparently, Stompanato made the mistake of pulling a gun on Connery on the set of the film. Connery promptly bent his hand back, and Johnny was forced to drop the weapon and flee with his tail between his legs. This account may lead some to swoon at the fictional James Bond acting like a real-life tough guy and a gentleman, running off Turner's abuser, but first consider Connery's own comments in ardent support of hitting women. He once told Barbara Walters in a video interview that 'it's not the worst thing to slap a woman now and then.' The police in London promptly deported Stompanato out of the country.

Lana decided to head to Mexico to relax after the incident, but on her way to a connecting flight she found that Stompanato was already on the plane. He went with her to Mexico, and according to her autobiography, he held her hostage there, verbally abusing her and repeatedly pointing a loaded gun at her, threatening her life.

The time in Mexico only ended because she got a Best Actress Oscar nomination for her work in the film *Peyton Place*. They returned to Hollywood by plane, so that Lana could prepare for the ceremony.

The 1958 Academy Awards Ceremony was the high and low point of Lana's life at that time. She recognised that it would be a poor idea to attend the Oscars with a known mobster, so she asked PR Agent Glen Rose to accompany her instead. This sent Stompanato into a rage, as he realised that she fully intended fully to keep him away from her Hollywood life.

On a rainy Good Friday, 4 April 1958, in a home that was being rented by Lana Turner at the time, Stompanato brought their situation to a fever pitch. Lana had previously kicked him out after he had threatened to cut her face up and kill her and her family. This wouldn't keep him away, however. Cheryl was down the hall and could overhear the confrontation. Cheryl went to the kitchen to get a knife and the subsequent series of events led to Stompanato being stabbed to death. He lay there, dead on the carpet, with the 14-year-old girl holding the weapon.

The police arrested Cheryl for the murder of the thug Johnny Stompanato. The murder weapon, and 8in knife, was found at the scene by the police – with no fingerprints on it. It was never made clear why the knife was apparently wiped of fingerprints, but this little detail would lead forever to speculation that perhaps Lana was the one wielding the knife that night, not her daughter. The pervasive theory was that Lana had contrived a story so that her daughter would take the fall for her.

The newspapers covered the story on their front pages. There were a variety of headlines out there, here are a few:

> 'Lana Turner's Daughter, 14, Kills Hoodlum'
> 'Film Star Tearful, Daughter Composed After Fatal Stabbing'
> 'Lana Turner's Daughter Slays Gangster Boy Friend of Mother'
> 'Lana Turner's Girl Kills Mother's Suitor'

There was an inquest into whether Cheryl would be brought up on criminal charges. It was 11 April 1958 and the Los Angeles courthouse where the testimonies were being heard was lined with video cameras from all of the major networks, from ABC to CBS. The entire situation was also broadcast live over the radio. All of America tuned in to see what would become of the knife-wielding daughter of one of their most beautiful stars.

Lana Turner took the stand and gave an emotional testimony about her relationship with Stompanato and the events of that fateful night the previous week. Turner broke down describing the nearly full year of abuse she endured at the hands of Stompanato. Her face was full of tears when she recalled that just before Cheryl had come to the room with a knife, Stompanato had grabbed a wire hanger from the closet and was threatening to thrash her face with it. Turner recalled, 'I said, "Don't ever touch me again. I am absolutely finished. This is the end. I want you out."'

It came out during the trial that Stompanato had died due to truly rare circumstances. There had been only one stab wound to his body and it had managed to sever his aorta.

It took only twenty-five minutes for the jury to return their verdict. It was found to be justifiable homicide. The decision of the courts and the court of public opinion, as we well know, are two very different things. Lana Turner had portrayed the murderous and unfulfilled wife in *The Postman Always Rings Twice* and there were many papers that chose to play off the image of her past roles and paint a shadow of doubt on the events of that evening in Beverly Hills.

Cheryl may have been found innocent of wrongdoing, but that didn't stop Stompanato's family filing a civil lawsuit. They tried to sue Lana Turner and Cheryl's father for $752,250, citing that parental neglect had led to Johnny's death. Turner settled for $20,000 to make the suit go away.

Cheryl's life did change after that. The juvenile courts took custody of her away from Lana and awarded it to Cheryl's grandmother. Cheryl's life subsequently took a dark turn; she was sent to reform school, engaged in drug use and alcohol, was arrested multiple times and eventually would have a year's stay in an institution. In 1988, Cheryl wrote her own book, titled *Detour*. It was during her time writing and researching this book that she reconnected with her mother and the two discussed many of their issues. Cheryl had come out as a lesbian to her mother and father as a teenager. She would eventually find her happiness and has been with her partner, and now wife, LeRoy, for many decades.

Later Life and Legacy

Lana Turner had lived quite a charmed life and had enjoyed a successful career until the homicide of Johnny Stompanato. In the years following the event, however, she had a lot of personal turmoil with her daughter, and faced a lot of rumour and innuendo from the public. This negative press could easily destroy a career in those days, but Turner found a way to prevail and raise from the ashes yet again. She would go on to star in Ross Hunter's remake of the film *Imitation of Life* in 1959. Her co-stars recount that the filming was very difficult for Turner. She had to take time off and was seen sobbing for days during certain scenes.

The filming of *Imitation of Life* may have proved challenging, but the aftermath would help re-establish Turner as a force to be reckoned with in Hollywood. She had wisely signed on for a 50 per cent stake in the film's profits. *Imitation of Life* brought in over $50 million at the box office, much of this may have been due to the movie being released only a year after the salacious homicide of her mobster boyfriend. The critical reviews of the movie were mixed, but one cannot argue with box office revenues.

Turner would go on to make films with Bob Hope and Dean Martin throughout the 1960s. Her 1961 film *By Love Possessed* became the first movie to be shown on a first class airline flight. Lana would marry three more times in the 1960s, so it was business as usual.

Lana would continue to work throughout the 1970s and part of the 1980s in various film and television roles. Her final role was a guest appearance on *The Love Boat* in 1985.

Lana was a product of her time, industry and circumstances. Her vices included very regular drinking, until her sixties, and a lifetime of smoking. It was the latter that would end up claiming her life on 29 June 1995. Lana had battled throat cancer, which eventually affected her jaw and lungs. She was 74 years old. Her remains were cremated and scattered in Hawaii.

Turner's star on the Hollywood Walk of Fame can be found on the North side of the 6200 block of Hollywood Boulevard.

Chapter Eight

William Desmond Taylor

Early LIfe

The man known as William Desmond Taylor was born on 26 April 1872 in Ireland. He would live a decent life in Ireland, attending college in England before emigrating to Kansas to work on a dude ranch. He was there to be trained as a gentleman farmer, but he instead discovered acting. Taylor would soon move to New York to pursue his newfound passion.

Career

Taylor began his career as an actor in 1913. He would soon graduate to directing his own films and that would take the primary spot in his heart. His career as a director would be prolific, as he helmed more than sixty movies in his day.

Taylor was considered 'The Gentleman Director' and was well respected by those in Hollywood. He would direct famous features, such as *Davy Crockett, Tom Sawyer, Anne of Green Gables, How Could You, Jean?, Huckleberry Finn* and *The Diamond From the Sky.*

Friendship with Mabel Normand

Taylor struck up a friendship with actress Mabel Normand (who has her own chapter in this book) that would last until the end of his life, almost to the hour. Normand loved Taylor and looked up to him. Taylor did his best to help her with her drug habits. He took her addiction very seriously, even reportedly threatening the drug dealers and trying to work with prosecutors to bring them to justice, hoping to keep Mabel away from them.

Mabel would often visit with Taylor, studying foreign language and discussing literature. He had taken her under his wing and was very hopeful for her recovery. There are rumours of a romantic relationship between the two, but this is more rumour than anything else, with neither ever confirming a sexual relationship.

Murder

It was one of the first Hollywood 'whodunit?' murders. It was the early hours of the morning on 2 February 1922 and Taylor's manservant, Henry Peavey, arrived for work at the usual time. He entered the home and found that the living room lights were already on. This wasn't a normal event, as the lights were always out when Mr Taylor went to bed and he was almost never up early. Peavey walked in and found Taylor's lifeless body lying on the floor.

When he discovered the grisly scene, Peavey immediately ran out into the courtyard and began screaming for help.

The police were called, but before they could arrive and secure the scene, the house was trampled through by neighbours and onlookers. This fact, unfortunately, greatly disturbed any forensic evidence that remained and complicated the ensuing murder investigation. Studio personnel showed up and took all kinds of documents, there were fingerprints everywhere and items were moved around.

The neighbours would later admit to the police that they had heard and seen some strange occurrences the night before, not realising what had transpired. Neighbour Faith McLean thought that she heard a car backfire. She looked out of her window and saw a figure on the porch of Taylor's home, draped in a trench coat with a turned-up collar to disguise their appearance. The conductor on nearby trolley car would corroborate this by stating a person matching that description got on his car around 8.00 pm.

One interesting theory involves another subject in this book, actress Mabel Normand. As noted, the two were close friends and Taylor spent the last evening of his life entertaining Normand in his home. Her chauffer drove her over, she arrived about 7.00 pm and stayed for less than an hour. The two had their normal interactions about foreign language, books and philosophy. Mabel left at approximately 7.45 pm. Taylor, ever the gentleman, walked her to the car to say their goodbyes. She went on her way home and not five minute later the shot was fired that ended Taylor's life. There were drugs involved when it came to Mabel. Taylor was after the drug-dealing gangsters that had roped in the innocent and naïve Mabel; he was set on confronting them. It is possible that the drug gangs eliminated him, but this is just a wild theory, as the police never found any evidence.

When Police searched Taylor's home after the murder they found a pink nightgown and a love letter from Mary Miles Minter, a then 19-year-old actress in silent films. Mary had one of the highest paid contracts of the era, worth over a million dollars. She was in love with Taylor, or so she professed. Her manipulative mother, Charlotte Shelby, completely controlled Mary's salary and career and so worked to put an end to the relationship. If the two had married, her mother would have lost control of her very large income. Mary's mother had been going to Taylor's office threatening him with everything from hat pins to guns. This came during a time of absolute sensationalism by the tabloids however, so it isn't a verifiable fact.

One evening, Mary's mother accused her of being intimate with Taylor; Mary took the family revolver and threatened to kill herself. Fifteen years after the murder, it is said bullets were found in her home that matched the murder weapon, so she at least owned the same kind of gun. The day before the body was found, mother and daughter argued again. Shelby is said to have overheard a phone conversation about the two eloping. She promptly locked her daughter in her bedroom and stormed out of the house in a rage. At the time of the murder she was at the family mansion with Carl Stockdale. Stockdale was himself an actor – one that had made the often impossible transition from silent film to talkies. It is claimed that he received $200 a week for the rest of his life from Shelby. This is, again, unverifiable hearsay.

Shelby herself was never actually questioned by the police, but this wouldn't stop the newspapers from picking up on her as a very possible suspect. The rumours would persist for many years. The 'word on the street' would be that she paid off the district attorney. In 1937, fifteen years after the death of Taylor, Shelby publicly demanded that a grand jury investigation be opened to hear the allegations against her, in order to clear her name. Mary took the stand and testified that her mother was innocent. Stockdale also took the stand, insisting that he was with Shelby that evening. Shelby's older daughter Margaret, however, took the stand and reportedly accused her mother of the murder and of paying off the district attorney.

There were various other theories about possible jilted lovers and angry husbands. None of these theories held a lot of water. That is until it was revealed that William Desmond Taylor wasn't actually William Desmond Taylor at all – he had a secret past life and his former valet, Edward Sands, had discovered it.

A Secret Life Revealed

Edward Sands worked for Taylor as a cook, valet and secretary. The summer before the murder Sands had forged cheques in Taylor's name while he was house sitting for Taylor. He is also said to have stolen jewellery and some other various valuables before skipping town and disappearing.

Taylor didn't hear from him again – until December 1921 when Sands sent a pawn ticket to Taylor in the post.

He had knowingly signed it Dean Tanner – the message was undoubtedly received in full.

William Cunningham Deane-Tanner was far from what one would have considered a gentleman or a stand-up guy. Tanner had deserted his wife and child in New York back in 1908 – fleeing west and changing his name. He was born in Ireland and had come to the United States as an immigrant. He soon married, became an antique dealer and had a daughter. He would later disappear without a trace. His poor family was left behind, convinced that their patriarch must have wandered off in a fit of amnesia. In 1912 his wife obtained a divorce based on his absence.

The exact path he took and his whereabouts between 1908 and 1913 aren't known. Unfortunately, Taylor didn't live long enough for him to ever reveal them in a memoir. We do know that by 1913 he had made his way to Los Angeles. He was using his new alias William Desmond Taylor to get work as an actor in silent films. Taylor quickly moved behind the camera, perhaps in an attempt to avoid his former family or friends ever seeing him alive and well at the picture shows. This would be a futile effort, because his wife and child would see him on the screen in the film *Captain Alvarez*. He eventually visited his daughter in 1921.

It has been conjectured that Sands was likely blackmailing Taylor at the time of his death. If Taylor had stood up to Sands, he may have come to confront him – leaving the famed director dead in the ensuing scuffle. This is, of course, just conjecture.

Legacy

'The gentleman director' will forever be remembered as a precursor to Steven Spielberg. He was the director with whom every actor wanted to work. His life ended in tragedy, but his legacy follows him. He does not currently have a star on the Hollywood Walk of Fame.

Taylor was laid to rest in a cathedral mausoleum crypt in the Hollywood Forever Cemetery. His tomb plate reads 'In memory of William C. Deane-Tanner. Beloved father.'

Chapter Nine

Joan Crawford

Early Life

The life of Joan Crawford began in the American southwest. Born Lucille Fay LeSueur on 23 March 1904, in San Antonio, Texas, she was the youngest of three children. Her older sister had died before Lucille's birth and her father, Thomas, abandoned the family before she was born. She wouldn't meet him for decades. A rocky start for a young girl, but her mother quickly married Henry Cassin. The Cassin family moved to Oklahoma and there he ran a vaudeville theatre. The fact that he was her stepfather wasn't revealed to her until she was older, she knew him only as daddy. The same man began to sexually abuse her when she was 11. The family had to move to Kansas City to escape the poor reputation Henry had made in Oklahoma. Lucille was enrolled in a Catholic school there under a scholarship and her mother divorced Cassin. Her stint at St Agnes Academy would last only three years, until the scholarship was up.

Lucille was then subjected to attending the less stately Rockingham Academy, which was okay until her stepfather stopped providing support and she had to work her way through the schooling. Crawford claimed later in life that the headmistress had physically and emotionally abused her during her time at the school. She was stuck working to pay her way through the school situation. It wasn't an uncommon situation in that era, many schools served as a sort of educational workhouse. She would graduate after four years of very hard work.

Crawford's Career

By the time she had graduated, Lucille was understandably looking for a way out of her current life. She wasn't cut out for academics and had a difficult time applying herself, so she pursued her childhood dreams of becoming a dancer and soon began to make her way as a chorus girl.

She was 19 and working on Broadway when she was discovered by Metro-Goldwyn-Mayer studios. Lucille got herself a screentest and a ride to Hollywood in 1925; it went well and she started playing bit parts in the silent movies, mostly as a flapper. The studio finally took notice of her after a year or so and felt that she needed a new name. The head of MGM publicity, Pete Smith, felt that her surname LeSueur reminded him of a sewer. It wasn't exactly a word that invoked beauty on the big screen.

A publicity stunt called 'name the star' was crafted. It was a genius way to engage and invest the public in this new screen starlet. The screen name that won was Joan Crawford. She reportedly hated her new moniker and thought it sounded too much like Crawfish.

Marriages and Affairs

Joan has been described as a difficult person to get along with. She was married a total of four times throughout her life; the first three marriages ended in divorce, while her fourth husband, Alfred Steele, passed away leaving Joan a widow for the rest of her days. Joan's first marriage was to a young Douglas Fairbanks Jr. She was 21 and he was just 19. The couple were young, but their marriage was far from a hurried affair. They were engaged for two years before tying the knot, managing to be a constant subject for the tabloids, who often speculated on whether they had married in secret during the two-year engagement.

Fairbanks once jokingly told the *LA Times*, 'Marriage is a wonderful thing, but it certainly scares you.' Though they would stay married for five years, they would never manage to find a true connection. Fairbanks' family felt that Crawford spent too much time narcissistically worrying about her own image and not enough time worrying about her marriage. It is said that both engaged in extramarital affairs during their half-decade of matrimony, so it is not surprising that the couple split in 1934.

Joan didn't wait long before she hurled herself into another commitment. Marriage number two came in 1935 when Joan wed actor Franchot Tone. The two had shared the screen many times and had a connection. Tone was very intellectual and artistic, characteristics that were new to Joan. He brought her into social circles that were foreign to her and provided her with new experiences. The couple tried to have children for years, but unfortunately all their attempts ended in miscarriage. The two divorced in 1939.

In 1942, Joan found love again. Husband number three was also an actor. Phillip Terry was a great prospect for marriage because he would not be shipped off to fight in the Second World War due to poor eyesight. The Hollywood 'it couple' spent the wartime era helping the troops through charitable causes such as the Victory Book Drive. Joan and Phillip parted ways in 1946.

It should be noted that somewhere in the thick of these marriages, particularly the earlier ones, Joan was engaged in a number of affairs. One of which was said to have been a more serious on-again, off-again tryst with none other than the great Clark Gable.

In 1955, Joan found love one final time, marrying the then head of PepsiCo, Alfred Steele. They eloped to Las Vegas on 10 May. During their time together, Steele managed to triple the profits of PepsiCo as the CEO of the company. A good number of Joan Crawford's films would later feature Pepsi product placements, which would come thanks to her role with Pepsi after the death of Steele in 1959. It is said that Joan really loved Alfred and was stricken with grief upon his death. She realised that the show must go on, however, and took a role in the Pepsi company, which paid $50,000 per year (approximately $434,000 today or £332,000) to make promotional appearances for the soda.

Children

Crawford had spent fifteen years at the top of the Hollywood elite, but suddenly she was hitting the point where her age was catching up with her and her once vibrant career was starting to fail. Joan decided that she wanted to adopt a child. She was found to be an unfit candidate for adoption in California, so she turned to the baby black-market in Nevada for a child. Joan would go on to adopt a total of five children. It would be her children that would create her most lasting controversy.

In 1940 Joan adopted Christina. Soon thereafter, she adopted a baby boy who she named Christopher, but he was reclaimed by his birth mother. In 1943, Joan adopted another boy and again named him Christopher. Two twin girls would follow in 1947, Catherine and Cynthia.

Christina has since conjectured that her mother used them for publicity to keep her in a positive light since she couldn't seem to hold a marriage together. It was said that she would dress the children up nice for photoshoots, and then not see them again for some time.

Christina says her little brother had it as bad as she did with her mother, as detailed in her tell-all book *Mommie Dearest*. In 1949 the children were both sent away to separate boarding schools.

Mommie Dearest

In what would, without a doubt, become her most lasting legacy, Joan Crawford is best known for being the wicked and abusive mother in the salacious tell-all book, titled *Mommie Dearest*. It isn't likely the note Crawford would have preferred to go out on, but nevertheless Joan's adopted daughter Christina felt compelled to tell the story of her horrific childhood. The book was penned and released within a year of Crawford's death in 1977, and it has been on the lips of the public ever since.

Mommie Dearest would remain on the *New York Times* bestseller list for forty-two straight weeks. The book would have been condemnation enough, but the accounts of child abuse would jump from the page onto the big screen; the film *Mommie Dearest* was made in 1981 with Faye Dunaway in the lead role as Joan Crawford. This mainstream attention would forever damn Crawford to be viewed as a monster in the public eye.

There is an entire memoir of complaints about an abusive and alcoholic mother in the book and it certainly deserves a read if you haven't yet had the opportunity. This is simply a taste of the types of accusations and accounts that you can expect in the pages of *Mommie Dearest*:

– Joan reportedly detested the use of wire hangers. Christina recounts one particular night where Joan woke her up in a rage and pulled her out of bed by her hair and beat her with a wire hanger, because her daughter had used one.
– Christina's account of the 'night raids' that would consist of a drunken Joan waking up the kids to make them clean at all hours of the night.
– The children were often restrained at night while in bed and Christina was occasionally forced to sleep in the shower.
– Christina was attacked by Crawford when she suspected her of attempting to seduce her fourth husband, Alfred Steele. That same husband mysteriously fell down the stairs to his death.

– Christina claims that Joan would strangle and hit them with various objects while drunk.
– The assertion is put forth that Joan cared more about her career than the children and that she may have adopted them as a publicity stunt to help her career, rather than out of any desire to be a parent.
– Joan once shredded Christina's favourite dress and then made her wear it to humiliate her.
– Christina was starved when she refused to eat uncooked meat that Joan was trying to force upon her.

The question remains as to whether or not the book is entirely accurate. There are some family and friends who have called it a work of fiction, while still others have made claims that it fits perfectly with what they knew and saw of Crawford. It is said that Crawford may have been aware of the book, which was already being written before her death. Interestingly, Christina and her brother Christopher were both left out of Crawford's will when she died.

Christina released an updated 20th Anniversary Edition of the book in 1998. The new edition contained an additional 100 pages of new material and edits out approximately fifty pages from the original book. The updated version concentrated more on Christina's relationship with Joan later in life.

Hollywood's First Sex Tape Scandal

It seems commonplace today in the current Hollywood landscape, but at the time no one had experienced a sex-tape scandal. It was a mistake that would haunt Crawford for the rest of her days. The tale involves blackmail, betrayal and a massive cover-up. The rumours of a Joan Crawford pornographic film had been persistent since she became famous.

The sad fact is that it was very common for women to turn to 'stag films' or revealing pictures in their early days of trying to 'make it' in showbusiness. It was a regular practice for photographers to refuse to take normal modelling pictures of women until they agreed to also take seedy 'alternate' photos for them to sell. The infamous cover of the first issue of *Playboy*, for example, features a nude image of Marilyn Monroe taken when she was still Norma Jean Baker. She had that image taken many years before and it was sold to Hugh Hefner by the photographer once Marilyn became famous.

It was flatly denied by Crawford in her own biography and by the movie studios, but many of her biographers agree that she did make at least two stag films, thought to be titled *Casting Couch* and *Velvet Lips*.

The star was blackmailed a handful of times by someone threatening to release the movies to the press. It is said that MGM knew about the films, saw them, and paid out a sum around $100,000. The worst part about the blackmail is that it is said to have been Joan's older brother who was responsible for it all.

Fortunately, the films were never released, saving her from experiencing the shame of public scrutiny, which would have undoubtedly been extremely harsh in those days.

The Feud with Bette Davis

It is one of the most storied and infamous feuds in Hollywood history. It is well known that there was no love lost between

Crawford and Bette Davis. The lingering question of why there was so much bad blood raises a lot of questions, but not many definitive answers.

The feud between the two certainly came to a head while they filmed the now cult horror film *What Ever Happened to Baby Jane?* In 1962, but there were persistent rumours about the two long before that particular clashing of the egos.

When Crawford eventually joined Warner Brothers she arrived on what had, up to that point, been the home turf of Bette Davis. The two were then the big league actresses under contract with Warner and found themselves competing for very similar roles. This may have been the beginning of the tension.

The idea of translating the book into a movie was actually Crawford's idea, as was casting Davis in the role opposite her. It could have been pure genius on Crawford's behalf, with the two stars aging and losing posture in Hollywood; how better to get a fantastic and realistic performance out of the film that features characters who are sisters entwined in a hateful and destructive relationship than to bring Davis into the fold. It wasn't difficult for the two professionals to channel their personal feelings into the film and it shows on the screen.

During the filming the personal issues between the two became legendary. It's said that Davis actually kicked Crawford during some of their more physical fight scenes.

One of the pivotal moments in the feud between the two screen legends centres around the 35th annual Academy Awards in 1963. The women both had Oscars to their name at that point and both were quite honestly hoping to be the first ever woman to win the honour of having three. Davis was the closest, having two wins to Crawford's one. The emotional and dramatic nature of *What Ever Happened to Baby Jane?* all but guaranteed that one or both of the women would get an Oscar nod. It turned out to be the case, but only Bette Davis got the nomination that year. The story goes that this made Crawford furious, although publicly she would play her part well, telling the press 'I always knew Bette would be chosen, and I hope and pray that she wins.' It was a very different story behind the scenes, however.

The legends state Crawford actively campaigned against Davis, convincing the other female nominees to allow her to accept their award on stage if they could not attend. It was more common in those days for actors not to be able to attend the awards if they were otherwise locked into a filming schedule, so they would choose someone else to accept the award on their behalf. Nominee Geraldine Page recalled her reactions when she was contacted by the legendary Crawford about the awards in the book *Bette and Joan: The Divine Feud*:

> I received a lovely note of congratulations from Miss Crawford ... And then she called me. I was tongue-tied, very intimidated in talking with her. To me she was the epitome of a movie star. I always loved her movies ... All I could manage was, 'Yes, Miss Crawford No, Miss Crawford.' When she mentioned about accepting the Oscar for me if I won, I said yes. Actually I was relieved. That meant I wouldn't have to fly all the way to California, or spend a lot of time

looking for a new dress to wear. I was happy and honoured that Joan Crawford would be doing all of that for me.

The winner of the award was Anne Bancroft for *The Miracle Worker*. Bancroft wanted Patty Duke to accept the award for her, but Duke was already nominated for another award, so she was unable to do it. Therefore, when the award was presented by Oscar winner Maximilian Schell, the camera panned backstage to show Miss Joan Crawford sauntering out to the stage to accept the Oscar on Bancroft's behalf. It was her ultimate snub to Davis, that her smiling face was there on stage to get the award of her competition.

In 1987, a decade after Crawford had passed away, Bette Davis spoke very candidly to Bryant Gumbel on the *Today* show about her relationship with Joan: 'As far as making the film with her, she was on time … she knew her line. She basically was a pro, but we're very different kind of women … very different kind of actresses.' Gumbel attempted to push further and get Davis to speak to the controversy between the two, but Davis was already speaking over him, perfectly willing to give her perspectives.

> Our parting of the ways came when she saw to it that I didn't get the Oscar for Baby Jane. She went to all the New York nominees and said 'If you can't get out I'll accept your award' and 'please do not vote for her'. She was so jealous. She was a fool my dear, we had great percentage. If I had won that Oscar, we'd have made a million more dollars

on the film, that's what always happens. So, she didn't ... she wasn't very smart about what she did.

Gumbel continues by asking Davis 'Are you hurt by the memory of that?' Bette thought for a moment, closed her eyes and revealed, 'I was furious, because that would have made me the first person with three. And as you know I always have to be first in everything. Yes, and I should have had it all.'

The 1963 Oscar nomination would prove to be the last for Davis and she would never become a three-time Oscar winner. That honour would instead go to Katharine Hepburn. Hepburn was not only the first woman to win three, but she has taken home four total Oscar wins, more than any other actor or actress in Hollywood, as of the writing of this book.

Her Death and Legacy

Joan eventually became a recluse until the time of her death in 1977. Alone in her Manhattan apartment, many conspiracy theories have suggested that she may have staged her death, so that she could even control her own demise.

Crawford gave away her beloved Shih Tzu, Princess Lotus Blossom, two days before she died of a myocardial infarction, commonly known as a heart attack. It wasn't surprising that Joan had to give up her dog, because she was feeling so ill due to her heart issues. The theory makes for a great story, but alas, in the end death simply comes for us all.

Chapter Ten

Barbara LaMarr

Early Life

It was back in 1896 that another star was born. Reatha Dale Watson, born to William and Rosana in the sleepy town of Yakima, Washington, would grow up to become an enigma, and a tragic vamp of the silver screen. Yakima had once shown a lot of promise in the settlement of the west, but the Northern Pacific Railroad had passed the town over, leaving the town occupants in a state of limbo from which they would take decades to recover.

Reatha's father had to travel all around the region to make his living as an editor in the newspaper business. A good portion of Watson's childhood was spent moving around to various cities in Washington and Oregon. Reatha would start her acting career at a young age, performing as the character Little Eva in a stage production of *Uncle Tom's Cabin* in Tacoma in 1904.

Reatha would gain a passion and love for the written word from her father. He would spend evenings reading tales of fantasy and poetry to his young family. William had an extensive collection of literature, in which his daughter would fully immerse herself. Her love for storytelling would drive her to a career in the new landscape of 'Hollywoodland' and the trappings that came with it. The family would experience a nomadic lifestyle for a few years, before finally putting roots down in Los Angeles. The timing and placement of Reatha's family would help to map out the rest of her illustrious, yet tragically short life story.

A Dramatic Start

An incident between the teenage Reatha and her estranged half-sister, Violet, would be the first known time that her life would take a dramatic turn. What actually happened is still in contention, but history confirms that a rather bizarre and intense situation took place. The setting was the early days of January 1913 in Los Angeles. A vulnerable 16-year-old Reatha had reportedly vanished from the family apartment at 12291/2 Figueroa Street. Her father rushed to inform the police that his innocent young daughter had been kidnapped by her half-sister and her companion, a man named C.C. Boxley. The tale that was spun in the local newspapers tells us that the innocent and doe-eyed girl went on a drive with the couple in their car up the San Fernando valley to visit Santa Barbara. She then learned on the road that they intended to take her to San Francisco and keep her there against her will. Then, just as bizarrely as she had vanished, Reatha suddenly reappeared a few short days later.

A warrant had been issued against the two for kidnaping and once they learned this they gave her money and sent her home with a cover story to keep them both out of trouble. This is one account of what happened, given by Reatha. When Reatha returned home she came armed with a story about how her estranged half sister and her vile, immoral boyfriend had tricked her into getting in their car and had whisked her away. The motivations were unknown, but assumed to be nefarious in nature. The couple were originally on the run, but eventually surrendered themselves by 7 January 1913. The attention had made Reatha a local celebrity and she relished the fact. When the police interviewed her they noted that she was far from traumatised by the alleged kidnapping, but was in fact gleeful and had quite enjoyed herself. The charges were soon dropped, as it was realised that she had likely been a willing participant in the trip.

Her Marriages

There is talk that Reatha was far from an innocent young girl, but had in fact been dancing in burlesque clubs since the age of 13, much to her father's chagrin. It is said that he tried to get juvenile courts involved to stop her behaviour. Her father was a huge influence on her and all the fantastical stories that he had read to her as a child sparked a creative energy in her mind, one that seemed to have a hard time understanding an appropriate time or place for her storytelling desires. She would eventually find her outlet in the burgeoning film industry, but her path would be a complicated one. Reatha would spend time working in vaudeville as a comedian and dancer, before finding her footing as an extra in a few silent films.

Reatha was reportedly married to a Jack Lytell from Yuma, Arizona, back in 1914, but he died of pneumonia only a few weeks into their marriage. Jack was a rancher and he had become entranced by Reatha, who had started going by the nickname of Beth by that point. The marriage reportedly took place in Mexico, so there is no official documentation to prove it, but she would return claiming to be the widow of Lytell, carrying his surname for many years.

A second, if extremely brief, marriage would come on 2 June 1914 to a man that she thought was named Max Lawrence. The two had a whirlwind romance and married rather quickly. It turned out that his name wasn't Max Lawrence at all, but was in fact Lawrence Converse. Converse had the complication of already being married with a family when he married Reatha under a fake name. The marriage was annulled a few days later, after he was accused of bigamy. He died from a clot on his brain just three days after they were married.

Reatha had a run of bad luck when it came to love so she took a couple of years off the marriage circuit, until she met a handsome and dapper vaudeville dancer named Phil Ainsworth. The two would marry in 1916. They became a husband and wife dance team, booking high-profile vaudeville stages thanks to Ainsworth's existing reputation and moved out to New York City to work. The two would eventually begin to argue over her spending habits and alleged attentions from other men; and were divorced by 1917.

Her fourth marriage was to a handsome Irish bloke named Nicholas Bernard Deely. A veteran of the vaudeville stage, he was eighteen years Barbara's senior. They married in 1918 and began touring together with his vaudeville troupe. During the throws of the First World War the couple entertained and lifted spirits all around America. Their career flourished for a short time, but soon the war was over and prohibition gained a grip over the nightlife of the country. When the alcohol disappeared, so did the cabaret clubs that they enjoyed working in. Suddenly, there was no work for a vaudeville troupe and when their careers began to fail, so too did their marriage. The couple would be divorced by 1921.

Her Career

> I could never be idle. I could never be merely a rich man's wife. I could never make my life out of the fabric of society.
>
> Barbara La Marr.

When her fantastic and romantic life as a performer came to a sudden halt, Barbara moved back in with her parents in their apartment. She was left with no good education or prospects, so out of a pure need she began to write. The young woman had already lived quite a life and had many experiences to draw from when engaging in her new creative outlet. She would find a new relationship with her father William during this time of her life, the two sitting together by the typewriter working on her stories. She had finally found an outlet that her father could understand and be proud of.

She was soon contracted to write six screenplays for the Fox Film Corporation. Although LaMarr and Deely were separated and living apart, he had begun working for Fox and it is assumed that he helped get eyes on her work. She began to find work as a screenwriter in 1920 and wrote under the name of Barbara La Marr Deely. Her writing credits include films, such as *The Mother of His Children, Rose of Nome, Flame of Youth* and *The Land of Jazz*. She was in a very good place in her life at this point, having felt that she had finally discovered her true calling.

Barbara worked feverishly throughout 1920 and 1921 on her films, but after a messy divorce and a heavy work schedule, she found herself without any further inspiration. She decided to take a break from her writing work. She had been living in Los Angeles with actress Marguerite De La Motte. She decided to accompany De La Motte to the set of her new film, starring opposite of Douglas Fairbanks Sr in the 1920 film *The Mark of Zorro*. Her decision to go to the set would change the entire trajectory of her life. Fairbanks was introduced to Barbara and thought her to be the most beautiful woman he had ever met. This would lead to him eventually casting her in his next film, titled *The Nut*. His wife, actress Mary Pickford, was especially attentive to La Marr. She would famously tell her that her beauty belonged in front of the camera, not behind it.

Her Baby and the KKK

In 1922, Barbara would give birth to her son Marvin, often calling him her 'little sonny'. The beginnings of their life together are a scandal that takes a good amount of time to unravel. It doesn't appear to be completely clear to this day. It was clear that Barbara's son would be her pride and joy. She expressed that she was going to raise him to be a good man, the kind of man that she had always been looking for, but could never find. She loved Sonny and hoped to see him grow into a fine young man. He would do that, but she would never live to see it.

The reality was that La Marr had a career in the film industry and by 1922 had been divorced four times. If she were pregnant she was then an unwed mother and therefore yet another example of the increasingly negative public perception of Hollywood, especially since the father was unknown.

Enter, millionaire and businessman Z.E. 'Zeke' Marvin. Marvin and LaMarr had met through mutual acquaintances. Zeke was a charitable man to be sure, but he was also the grand titan of the Dallas chapter of the Ku Klux Klan. The Klan, infamous for their hateful and often violent actions towards minorities, had a major presence at that time in the southern parts of the United States. Marvin had donated a whopping $50,000 to help give a home to an orphanage, called Hope Cottage. It was here that La Marr would apparently give over her actual birth child, so that an adoption could be staged. Zeke Marvin took La Marr to the orphanage and helped to orchestrate the entire charade, having the orphanage staff name the baby Marvin, so they would know exactly who he was when La Marr staged her tour of the orphanage. She adopted her own son and presented herself as a saint to the public, who ate up the fake story. It would help La Marr maintain a more wholesome image as a charitable mother, helping her career to continue to thrive.

La Marr's Turmoil

A lot has been written about La Marr and her battles with everything from an eating disorder to drug and alcohol abuse. These wouldn't be shocking issues to find in Hollywood today, but during the silent film era they were kept very quiet by the studios. It's important to note that there is no definitive proof that she was involved in any of these illicit activities, but it does continue to be the accepted history of her young life. There is also a desire by many to tear down successful young women with rumour and insult to their character, and that is possibly what was done here.

The reality was that she was becoming visibly more sickly, but this could also have been from undiagnosed physical ailments that had nothing to do with drugs or alcohol abuse. Barbara was known to sleep only two hours a night, not wishing to waste any of her life by sleeping. This lack of sleep could easily cause emotional and physical distress that is difficult to measure.

In 1926, while filming *The Girl from Montmartre*, La Marr had lost a significant amount of weight, giving her a sickly appearance and causing worry to those on the set. Eventually, she was unable to complete the film due to illness. She left many scenes unfinished upon her departure. The show, as they say, must go on, so her scenes were finished by a lookalike named Lolita Lee. This would prove to be her final appearance in a film.

Death

> Hello, everybody! I'm getting better … I'll be all
> right pretty soon.
>
> Barbara La Marr

Barbara La Marr would meet her end on 30 January 1926, at her home in Altadena, California. She was suffering from tuberculosis and nephritis, which is an inflammation of the kidneys. The once glamorous and vulnerable silent-screen vixen died at the age of 29. The newspapers would do their best to sensationalise the tragedy, blaming her death on a variety of absurd notions from complications caused by extreme diets, or a nervous breakdown. The reality wasn't quite so fascinating. In reality, Barbara was a very ill young woman who lived an unfortunately short life. Her Hollywood myth lives on, but it's her true story that deserves attention.

La Marr would make arrangements on her deathbed for her friends ZaSu Pitts and her husband Tom Gallery to adopt and raise her son. The couple would take Marvin in as their own and rename him Don Gallery. Don would grow up to be a fine man, with a loving home. Don would tell stories of his mother keeping cocaine and heroin in the house, but he would admit late in his life that he had no recollection of his birth mother and only knew the love of Pitts and Gallery.

The *Los Angeles Times* reported on the funeral in the next day's paper. The scene was a mob, with thousands of adoring fans and curious citizens gathering outside of the Walter C. Blue Undertaking Chapel hoping to have a look at La Marr's casket as it made the final journey to burial. The police struggled to maintain over the crowds and as Barbara's body was placed into the hearse for transport to the cemetery, hordes surrounded the vehicle. In the midst of the kerfuffle, it was reported that no less than five women fainted and were trampled. The crowd poured into the funeral home, even as the hearse exited, hoping to find any remnant of her funeral, but all items had already been removed, down to the flowers.

Legacy

Barbara La Marr was one of the first superstars and remains a Hollywood legend. Her body was put to rest in the Hollywood Forever Cemetery, where it lies to this day. Her headstone features her screen name of Barbara La Marr and reads quite simply 'With God Is The Joy And Beauty Of Youth'. You can find Barbara's star on the Hollywood Walk of Fame, situated on the west side of the 1600 block of Vine Street.

Chapter Eleven

Mabel Normand

Early Life

Mabel Normand was a goddess of the silver screen. She was a contemporary of Charlie Chaplin and Fatty Arbuckle who would move beyond the realms of acting into directing and producing her own features with her own company. Her star wouldn't shine for long, however, as she would only make it to the age of 38.

She was born Amabel Ethelfreid Normand in New York on 10 November 1893. Her father worked as a stage carpenter and cabinetmaker. She was described as a very wild child with an adventurous spirit. As a youth she was a champion swimmer and would regularly swim the Hudson River.

Career

In 1908, at the age of 14, she was paid to model dress patterns for Butterick's clothing in Manhattan. The pay was fifty cents an hour, which is the equivalent to around $12 (or £9.36) an hour today. To provide a bit of context, $12 an hour would be more than the starting wage at Walmart in America in 2018. It was a good wage for a young girl to be making, but it was only the beginnings of a career.

Mabel would soon meet an artist by the name of Charles Dana Gibson, for whom she would model hats and pose for postcards. You may remember Gibson as the man who pioneered his famous 'Gibson Girls'. The work was solid, but the pay still wasn't up to the level that Mabel would need to make her way in the world.

Mabel was a major player in the early days of the silent film era. She was one of those close to mogul Mack Sennett at his Keystone Studios. She lit-up the silver screen, starring in films opposite some of the biggest names of the era, such as Fatty Arbuckle and Charlie Chaplin.

Normand met Sennett while still living in New York, before he left for Hollywood to find his fortune. Senet had convinced a 16-year-old Mabel that she needed to star in the pictures. The two would take up as co-workers and lovers. Eventually, he would leave her heartbroken as he went out west to make movies in 1909. It wouldn't be the last time that the lives of the two would intersect.

Having made her mind up to explore the world of silent films, Normand got her first role from D.W. Griffin in 1910. She was paid a lofty $10 an hour to be in the pictures, a major pay raise compared to her modelling work. In today's money that would be the equivalent of approximately $250 (£194) an hour. She became a member of the Vitagraph Studios comedy troop and began delighting audiences almost immediately. She ventured out to Hollywood to work for her ex-boyfriend, Sennett, in 1912 at the age of 19.

When working for Mack Sennett she portrayed the 'damsel in distress' in many of the Keystone Cops films. Not only was she a beauty, Mabel would work hard for a living, doing stunts like horse riding, hot-air ballooning and being dragged through the mud by rope. One of her most successful film pairings would be with Fatty Arbuckle, with whom Normand would make twenty-six films. They had a chemistry that was fun and charming, and the opposite nature of their respective looks would serve as a template for situation comedy for decades to come. Mabel was acting for a living and having the time of her life.

It was during her time at Keystone Studios that Mabel met a young comedian named Charlie Chaplin. In his autobiography Chaplin admits that he had fallen wildly in love with Normand, but she did not feel the same way. It wasn't the first, nor would it be the last, time that her beauty and charm gained Normand an admirer.

Mabel turned a lot of heads, but alas her heart still belonged to Mack. It was an affection that he would never fully return. The two had planned to marry in the summer of 1915, but their engagement was brought to a sudden end when Mabel walked in on Mack sleeping with her protégé, actress Mae Busch. Mack went to great lengths to try and make the indiscretion up to Mabel, letting her produce and direct a film on her own. He even built her a dedicated studio as an apology. The Mabel Normand Feature Film Company would end up producing only one film, a silent movie named *Mickey*.

In 1916, age 23, she worked on *Mickey* with complete creative control. Money problems held up release of the film for two years, but once she was finally able to release it in 1918, *Mickey* was a huge success. Mabel, seeing an opportunity, turned the delay into a public relations stunt to promote the film and created huge public anticipation. Not only was *Mickey* a huge hit, the title song 'Mickey' was also a hit, making it one of the first songs from a movie to find mainstream success.

When Mabel was 26 she had finally had enough of dealing with Mack and left his grip, signing with Goldwyn; soon she was earning a whopping $4,000 a week, which would equate to around $60,000, or £46,500, today.

The murder of William Desmond Taylor

The story of Mabel Normand intersects with that of another subject in this book, director William Desmond Taylor. She was the last known person to see him alive. The two were reportedly friends and he was giving her French lessons. There is also talk that he was trying to help her get clean and away from the control of the Hollywood drug dealers. During her time with Goldwyn studios Mabel began to fall apart, partying excessively and apparently taking drugs, and Taylor was trying to help her find the right path by getting her into a drug rehab clinic.

She spent less than an hour in Taylor's Hollywood home that fateful evening of 21 February 1922. He walked her to her car, where her driver was waiting, and saw her off. That was the last time anyone would see him alive. When the story broke, the press weren't interested in the truth, they were more interested in rumour and gossip. One rumour even suggested that Taylor was providing her with drugs, but the opposite was true. Taylor was doing his best to help Normand find herself through education.

Mabel was interrogated by the police regarding Taylor's death, but was not charged with any crime. The mystery murder was never solved and the scandal brought Mabel a lot of undesirable publicity and questions about her personal character.

It wasn't long before she was involved in yet another scandal. On New Year's Day 1924 she spent the afternoon getting drunk and partying with friends. Mabel's personal chauffeur was supposed to watch over her and take her home if she had drunk too much and was out of control. He tried to protect her and take her home, but found resistance from a wealthy playboy named Courtland Dines.

The details of exactly what happened that evening were never made clear. The story from everyone involved kept changing. All we know for certain is that Dines was in his Los Angeles apartment with Mabel and her friend, silent film actress Edna Purviance. Dines and the chauffeur had a confrontation which ended with Dines being shot in the chest with a gun that belonged to Normand. The case was brought to trial, but Dines refused to testify so the chauffeur was acquitted of all charges. The real details of the story may never be known.

This would cause quite the scandal for Mabel, because it was during the prohibition era and the three were known to have been drunk. She was on the front page yet again, having her wholesome screen image tarnished by her private life. The American public was sick of Hollywood scandal, with the whole lot apparently constantly engaged in untoward dealings. Mabel would have trouble playing her usual beloved character on the screen after that point.

Death

The last part of Mabel's career would see a return to working with Hal Roach. She was signed to his studios in 1926. She would also marry a fellow actor named Lew Cody, whom she had met while working on the set of *Mickey*.

Mabel would succumb to the effects of tuberculosis on 23 February 1930 at the age of 38. Her funeral service was held in Los Angeles at the Church of the Good Shephard in Beverly Hills. The pallbearers at her funeral included the likes of Charlie Chaplin, Douglas Fairbanks Sr, D.W. Griffith, Mack Sennett, Louis B. Mayer, Sidney Patrick Grauman and Samuel Goldwyn.

Normand was laid to rest by her husband as Mabel Normand-Cody at the Calvary Cemetery in Los Angeles.

Her Legacy

Mabel Normand may not be a household name in the modern era, like Charlie Chaplin, but she also hasn't had the benefit of a glamorous Hollywood biopic to bring her into popular culture. That isn't to say she has been forgotten. There are various websites dedicated to her life and career and you can find playlists of her films on popular websites like YouTube. Hopefully new generations can still find her film-work this way and enjoy the gifts she left behind. Mabel has a star on the legendary Hollywood Walk of Fame at 6821 Hollywood Boulevard.

Chapter Twelve

Roscoe 'Fatty' Arbuckle

Scandal has become synonymous with Hollywood, but there was a time when the silver screen was yet untouched by the wicked deeds of its larger-than-life stars. The first major scandal to rock a Hollywood superstar was that of Fatty Arbuckle and a the murder of a young woman named Virginia Rappe.

In the post-First-World-War era, films became the most popular new medium and Arbuckle was one of the biggest stars of the silent screen. Roscoe 'Fatty' Arbuckle was one of the highest paid actors in Hollywood in his day. The heavy-set comedian was a man of many talents, enjoying work not only as an actor, but also as a screenwriter and director. The charming funny man had no trouble getting regular high-profile work until the time of his death in 1933, but the legacy that he left after his death at the age of 46 is stained with scandal, suspicion and allegations of rape and murder of the actress Virginia Rappe. The accusations came after one night in 1921, when Rappe met her untimely demise. A whopping three legal trials followed and Fatty was soon shunned from the industry, his films banned, and he was forced to work under an alias. Did Arbuckle parlay his fame into a 'get out of jail free' card, like so many celebrities do to this day, or was it all just a huge misunderstanding? In order to understand what really transpired, we need to understand the man behind the scandal.

Early Life

Roscoe Conkling 'Fatty' Arbuckle was born in Smith Center, Kansas, on 24 March 1887. Arbuckle was one of nine children and the man who would become known as 'Fatty' later in life was born at the hefty weight of 13lb (almost 6 kg)! Arbuckle would unfortunately be introduced to violence at a young age. His father was an alcoholic, and that brought physical abuse to the family. He was especially hard on Roscoe, whom he believed might not be his biological son.

Roscoe's family moved out to California when he was just a toddler and it was there that his career on the stage would begin. Arbuckle's mother, Mollie, saw talent in her little boy, who displayed quite the singing voice, and pushed him into performing on stage. The life of young Roscoe would come crashing down when his beloved mother died in 1899. Roscoe was only 12 at the time. In the aftermath, his stern father wasn't interested in indulging his aspirations to the stage like his mother had. His father soon abandoned the 12-year-old Roscoe.

It was time for Roscoe to grow up and start fending for himself if he was going to survive. He got a job at a hotel and was discovered there by one of the patrons who heard him singing and dancing about while doing his work. They convinced him to try out for a talent show. Arbuckle made a huge impression at the show, but not the way that he had initially hoped. He had been a fan of vaudeville since he was a boy, but he could rarely afford to attend the shows. This was his chance to be a part of it, but the husky talent wasn't cutting it on the vaudeville stage and that notorious shepherd's crook began to emerge from the side of the stage to pull him off, so the next act could have a chance. Arbuckle reacted the only way he could think of and he literally did a somersault off of the stage into the orchestra pit. The crowd roared with approval and the idea of 'Fatty' was born in Roscoe's mind. Fatty toured with his vaudeville troupe for the next decade.

Career

He was one of the most famous faces in Hollywood, marked with a larger stature that wasn't nearly as common then as it is now. Fatty was friends and contemporaries with major names that still resonate today, such as Charlie Chaplin and Buster Keaton.

Fatty would take his slapstick character with a physical comedy element on the road and soon he was offered work at various theatres and vaudevillian troupes around the west coast of America. Arbuckle married actress Minta Durfee on 6 August 1908. The visual of the two is like a stereotypical sitcom couple that is often shown on television to this day. There was Fatty – a large and husky husband (this one weighing in around 266lb in his prime) and an attractive wife who is shorter in stature and slim. The visual dichotomy of Minta and Roscoe next to each other was as comical as many of their films.

The history books tell us that in 1913 Arbuckle was first hired by the infamous Mack Sennett Studios to be a part of the now legendary troop of the Keystone Cops. Thanks to recently uncovered Motion Picture Studio Directory and Trade Annuals from 1919 and 1921, we know that Fatty actually started with Sennett's Keystone Studios as an extra. The excerpt from the trade reads: '...screen career, began with Keystone, 1913, as an extra man at $3 per day; advanced to regular parts; later played leads and became director; directing and acting for nearly 3 yrs...'.

Sennett eventually saw a need for more individual characters within the cops, and Fatty's weight got Mack's attention. Sennett recounts their first meeting with shock and awe at the charisma and physical tumbling ability that Arbuckle displayed, especially considering his size. There are some stories that surround their first meeting where Sennett claims that Arbuckle introduced himself as 'Fatty', and yet others that assert that Arbuckle loathed the nickname and that it was given to him by Sennett Studios.

Although he started with Keystone at the bottom and worked up to one of the famous Keystone Cops, Arbuckle would become most famous for his romantic comedy films with the lovely Mabel Normand. The two would become a favourite of audiences, largely due to their contrasting appearance. It would become a blueprint for comedy movies and television, inspiring shows like *The Honeymooners* and even modern day series like *The King of Queens* and *The Simpsons*. This time-tested formula is one of the more lasting of Arbuckle's entertainment legacy.

It was Arbuckle's overweight appearance that gave him an edge in the entertainment industry and set him apart from his contemporaries. The idea that 'fat is funny' was a pervasive thought at the time. Not one to rely on his size for laughs, Fatty made sure that he was just as limber and physical as other silent film comedy actors of the era. It's no coincidence that in 1918 Fatty was the first actor in Hollywood to earn a million-dollar salary. Although Charlie Chaplin began earning a million dollars in the same year as Fatty, that was for his own studio producing films, not just for starring in them.

In 1917 Arbuckle had started his own production company, which he dubbed 'Comique'. This vital step in his career would see him not only produce fourteen films, but would also pair him with the now legendary Buster Keaton. Arbuckle was a mentor to Keaton and the duo would become firm friends, remaining that way for the rest of their lives. The offer of a three-year contract for $1 million per year was just too big a draw for Arbuckle and he would sell his shares in Comique to Keaton in 1919, accepting Paramount's contract. It was a new era for Fatty, one that would prove to be very lucrative, and ultimately destructive to his future as a performer.

There was a time when Fatty Arbuckle was nearly as famous and popular as Charlie Chaplin, but he is hardly a household name and is rarely spoken of in the same vein as the slapstick legend. One of the reasons that we don't see Arbuckle canonised in the annals of cinematic history to the extent of Chaplin is the horrific nature of his very public scandal. Nearly a century later, we take a look at the evening of 11 September 1921. Long before 11 September became forever linked to the attack on the Twin Towers in New York City, the date was associated with the massive scandal that would lead to the arrest of beloved funny man Roscoe 'Fatty' Arbuckle by the San Francisco Police Department, for the rape and murder of Virginia Rappe.

The Young Actress

Virginia Rappe was the epitome of a then modern Jazz-age woman. She was liberal, unmarried and free-thinking. Rappe was a model and a fashion designer during a time when the fashion industry was truly in its infancy. She came to Hollywood to find her future and in doing so became immersed in the world of motion pictures. We will never know if Rappe would have become a success, because she died so young. A supporting actress, she was given only bit parts in silent films. Her name would go down in the history books, but not for her art.

A talented young woman, Virginia was also a product of her era. The conservative politicians of the day had taken control with their forced alcohol prohibition and thus emerged a prolific subculture of secret drinking clubs and parties. These were often debaucherous scenes full of drugs, booze and illicit sex.

A Murder?

It was Labour Day weekend in the year 1921 and there was a fantastic alcohol party planned in the lush suite in room 1219 at the San Francisco St Francis Hotel. Fatty had been hard at work, filming three movies back to back, and it was time for him and his friends to cut loose and enjoy themselves over the holiday weekend. It was time to enjoy some of the fruits of his $1 million dollar per year contract and indulge in drinking, dancing and partying.

Arbuckle would spend the next few days in his pyjamas, enjoying the debauchery and the bootleg hooch. The party took place during the first year of America's thirteen-year Prohibition era, so when the public learned of the illicit party, the fact that alcohol was involved would weigh heavily on their opinion of Fatty.

It was a few days into the party, when they began to run low on alcohol. Fellow actor and director Freddy Fishback was elected to venture out into the world of sobriety and procure some more booze for the partygoers. When Freddy was out he ran into the pretty young actress Virginia Rappe and invited her back to the party. This one event would change the fates of everyone involved forever.

What unfolded next is in dispute, and varies greatly depending on which eyewitness account you believe. The undeniable facts are that Rappe came back to the hotel party with Freddy. She would be declared dead on 9 September 1921, due to a ruptured bladder and secondary peritonitis.

Initial testimony about the death from partygoers seemed to incriminate Fatty Arbuckle in the death of Rappe. One particular attendee, Maude Delmont, made it very clear that she felt Fatty had been inappropriate in his aggressive pursuit of Rappe throughout the day and would tell the papers that he was, undoubtedly, directly responsible for her death.

Fatty initially told reporters that Rappe had consumed too much alcohol and had become hysterical, complained that she was unable to breathe and proceeded to tear off her clothing. This statement, however, would change by the time Fatty testified in court.

It wasn't long before Arbuckle was arrested, booked and held without bail at the San Francisco Hall of Justice. Fatty had turned himself in to the police and was now sitting snugly in cell number twelve in their felony row. The police released his mug shot, showing an understandably grim view of the typically jovial star.

The Trials

The preparation of what would have been considered a proper defence for Fatty Arbuckle during that era followed. It consisted of an offensive barrage of claims about Virginia's character. It remains a travesty that is still perpetrated in courtrooms to this day, because sexual assault is the only crime where the victim is put on trial and held under a veil of suspicion. There was talk of her reputation as a party girl and a drinker, known to take off her clothing at parties and be promiscuous in her dealings with men. There were even those that accused her of being a prostitute; all claims that are easy to throw around about a victim who wasn't alive to defend her character.

The testimony of a few of the witnesses are said to have changed drastically between the time that they met with the District Attorney and when they actually arrived in court. It was alleged at the time that witness intimidation had been involved, which isn't beyond the realms of possibility. Fatty Arbuckle was a huge meal ticket for the studios and a very powerful player in Hollywood. Imagine you're a young actress and the future of your career may hinge on how you remember the events of one day. This same kind of mental intimidation was utilised to shelter abusers like movie producer Harvey Weinstein in the modern era, so the possibility that this was employed during a time when Hollywood had far less accountability isn't too far out.

The First Trial: 14 November to 4 December 1921

It was the trial of the century. The court was expecting large crowds, so they prepared by stationing twelve armed police in and around the courtroom and admission to the trial was tightly monitored. When Fatty had his initial hearing, only women were allowed in the room, because they were holding him in the women's department of the police court. The trial, however, allowed both men and women to attend.

Notably missing from the trial was the damning testimony of Maude Delmont. It was determined that her personal reputation was far too sketchy to allow her on the stand. A lot of the motivation for the District Attorney to pursue Arbuckle was derived from her account of the events. Unfortunately, Delmont had been involved in a number of illegal activities herself, including blackmail. This wasn't surprising, as the list of criminal activity associated with many of the partygoers was extensive. This was, after all, an illegal booze party. We know that many involved in Hollywood back in this era (and often even today) were heavily connected to the underworld and criminal activity. It was determined that the defence would have no trouble discrediting her character and casting a shadow of suspicion upon her motivations. It was thought that she may have had blackmail in mind, with the idea to use her story to extort money from the funny man. This doesn't hold a lot of weight in rational thinking, since she was quick to go public with her claims and testimony, leaving no room for extortion on her behalf. Unfortunately, the possibility was enough to keep her off the stand. Her reputation aside, it didn't mean that her account of the events was necessarily untrue.

The jury would come back deadlocked and so Fatty would be fated to stand trial a second time.

The Second Trial: 11 January to 3 February 1922

The next trial began almost a month after the end of the first. There weren't many details that would change in the presentation of the case. The prosecution would keep the same arguments, while the defence would still rely upon their initial statements. Even the judge presiding over the trail was the same. The jury is all that really changed – and yet the more things change, the more they stay the same.

During this trial the character of the district attorney would be called into question. There were a few witnesses who would take back their testimony, stating that he had pressured them into lying. This could certainly have been the case, although since the movie studios were closely tied to the mob in these days it is also possible that certain pressures were applied. No one will ever know for certain.

There was no closing argument made by the defence for Arbuckle and he never took the stand. This move would lead many to be convinced of his guilt. This trial would last less than a month. The jury would come back after five days – again with a deadlock. This second mistrial wouldn't be the end of the legal ordeal for Fatty, because there was yet another trial in his future.

The Third Trial: 13 March to 12 April 1922

The third and final trial for Arbuckle began a month after the second. The previous six months saw Fatty spending time in prison – far from his usual lavish lifestyle. He was put through trial after trial and with all of the coverage from the newspapers, his public persona was completely ruined. It would not matter what the verdict was in this trial, the court of public opinion already viewed him as a disgusting and perverse man – and this would shine a negative light on much of Hollywood, as well. Fatty's films were beginning to be banned in many places and any traces of a career were long gone.

This time around the defence decided to play it more aggressively, working hard to discredit the prosecutions witnesses and going after those involved more thoroughly. There was one witness missing and a lot more dirt had been dug up on Virginia's past, which was used callously by the defence. Arbuckle did take the stand this time, hoping for a positive response from the jurors.

The Final Verdict

On the afternoon of 12 April 1922, the third and final jury to decide Fatty's fate returned with a verdict after only a short six-minute-long deliberation. He was acquitted on all charges Arbuckle chose to issue a statement following the verdict, it read as follows:

> This is the most solemn moment of my life. My innocence of the hideous charges preferred against me has been proved by a jury of the best men and women in San Francisco—fourteen in all—rendering a verdict immediately after the trial. For this vindication I am truly grateful to God and my fellow men and women.

The jury felt so strongly about their verdict, and at the effect the three trials had taken on the life and career of Fatty Arbuckle that they chose to release a public statement through the press, hoping to smooth over the immense damage that had been done to his reputation.

> Acquittal is not enough for Roscoe Arbuckle. We feel that a great injustice has been done to him. We feel that a great injustice has been done him. We feel also that it was only our plain duty to give him this exoneration, under the evidence, for there was not the slightest proof adduced to connect him in any way with the commission of a crime. He was manly throughout the case and

told a straightforward story on the witness stand, which we all believed.

The happening at the hotel was an unfortunate affair for which Arbuckle, so the evidence shows, was in no way responsible.

We wish him success and hope that the American people will take the judgment of fourteen men and women who have sat listening thirtysome days to the evidence that Roscoe Arbuckle is entirely innocent and free from all blame.

Fatty banned from the big screen – the last decade of his life and death

The trials weren't the end of Fatty's problems, because regardless of how the jury found him, a lot of details about his private life had been made public. The bubble of privacy was burst and many Hollywood stars were now being seen as immoral – far from the often pure and lighthearted characters that they were portraying on the big screen.

On 18 April 1922 the Motion Pictures Producers and Distributers of America (MPPDA) would hand down a ban on Fatty. This newly formed censorship committee would find that Fatty was of 'poor morals'. Will H. Hays, who was the head of the MPPDA, banned Fatty from working in the motion pictures again. His films were also thus officially banned from ever being shown.

The ban would only last until the end of that year, because the public outcry was clear that it was too far of a measure.

This lifting of the ban wouldn't help Fatty find work, however. No one wanted to hire him, fearing that he would do more damage than good for the studios. Fortunately for Fatty, his good friend Buster Keaton would share some of his profits with him, helping to ease his burdens.

The final decade of Fatty's life signalled a new era for the former star. He was finally able to return to Hollywood, but this time it would be a role behind the camera. Fatty found work again, but as a director and under an assumed name – William B. Goodrich. He would pump out dozens of comedies over the ensuing decade.

Photoplay magazine would run an article in support of Fatty in 1925, stating:

> I would like to see Roscoe Arbuckle make a comeback to the screen. The American nation prides itself upon its spirit of fair play. We like the whole world to look upon America as the place where every man gets a square deal. Are you sure Roscoe Arbuckle is getting one today? I'm not.

Fatty's wife, Minta, divorced him in 1923 and the two remained good friends. He found love again when he married Doris Deane in 1925. The relationship would end poorly four years later, with her accusing Fatty of desertion and cruelty. In 1932 Fatty would give marriage a go one last time, marrying actress Addie Oakley Dukes McPhail. The marriage would only last a year, because Fatty wasn't long for this world.

Death

On 29 June 1933, at the age of 46, Roscoe died peacefully in his sleep from a heart attack. Earlier that very same day, he had signed a new contract with Warner Brothers to get in front of the camera again as a comedic actor in a feature film. Enough time had passed since the scandal, and Hollywood was finally ready to take a chance on Fatty again. Unfortunately for him, he was never able to fulfil the contract.

Fatty had passed away while in New York. He was cremated and his ashes scattered at sea in the Pacific Ocean.

Legacy

The greatest legacy that Fatty left behind was the scandal that plagued him. We will never know what happened that night in suite 1219, but the aftermath left a young woman with a promising life ahead of her dead, and a beloved actor forever shamed in the eyes of the public that once adored him.

Fatty does have a star on the legendary Hollywood Walk of Fame. It can be found on the North side of the 6700 block of Hollywood Boulevard.

Chapter Thirteen

Clara Bow

Clara Bow was Hollywood's 'It' girl, reigning on top of the world for a time, until her nervous breakdown and public scandals drove her away from the industry that made her a star.

Early Life

Clara Gordon Bow was born on 29 July 1905 in Prospect Heights, Brooklyn, New York. Their family apartment was a one-room shanty above a church. Clara was a miracle to her parents, because two previous daughters had died in infancy. Robert and Sarah Bow were warned not to try and have more children, but their final attempt was successful and the world was given Clara. Her young life, unfortunately, would be anything but charmed.

Her father had trouble finding work and was often absent from their lives. Her mother suffered from epilepsy and her moods became increasingly violent. According to the Epilepsy Foundation,

> It is now believed that most people with epilepsy are
> no more likely than others to act aggressively. A few
> do have episodes of aggressive behaviour between

seizures (interictal aggression). Researchers have proposed that there are syndromes of interictal behaviour changes that can occur in people with epilepsy.

Clara often felt that she was taking care of her mother, rather than the other way round. There was an incident in February of 1922, where Clara's mother held a knife to her throat while she was sleeping. Her mother couldn't remember doing it the next day, but it led to her being committed. It was now just Clara and her father – which would make for disastrous results.

When Clara was 16 years old her father began to rape her. There is some conjecture about whether this was a new situation or whether it had been going on prior to this time. In that same year, 1921, the beautiful young girl would win a bit-role in a silent film by entering a 'Fame and Fortune' beauty contest in a magazine. The magazine wrote of their winner:

> She is very young, only 16. But she is full of confidence, determination and ambition. She is endowed with a mentality far beyond her years. She has a genuine spark of divine fire. The five different screen tests she had, showed this very plainly, her emotional range of expression provoking a fine enthusiasm from every contest judge who saw the tests. She screens perfectly. Her personal appearance is almost enough to carry her to success without the aid of the brains she indubitably possesses.

The actual prize was simply a gown and a trophy – with a promise that she would be introduced to the right people in Hollywood and in 1922, Clara appeared in *Beyond the Rainbow*. Movies were Clara's escape from the horrors of her childhood and would devote herself to them fully. Clara would look back upon her childhood with disdain:

> No one wanted me in the first place. Often I was lonesome, frightened and miserable. I never had a doll in my life. I never had any clothes, and lots of times didn't have anything to eat. We just lived, and that's about all. Girls shunned me because I was so poorly dressed – the worst looking kid on the street. I decided that girls weren't any good, and being lonely and needing child friends, cast my lot with the neighborhood boys. I became a regular tomboy – played baseball, football and learned to box.

Career

Clara would start to get work in the silent movies, with her first breakout role coming in the film *Down to the Sea in Ships* in 1923. This would lead to a few more roles, but the big one would come when she was cast as the 'tomboy' in the F. Scott Fitzgerald written film, *Grit*. *Variety* magazine would hail her as a powerful presence on the screen, stating that she 'lingers in the eye, long after the picture has gone'. She would stay in New York, acting for a few months under contract before leaving her father and her life there behind for Hollywood in July of 1923. It was a new start for Clara, far from the painful memories of her past.

Clara was nothing if not a dedicated workaholic. She would commit to a rigorous work schedule, not leaving herself much time for anything else. When she did have free time, she would party. She was under contract to Preferred Pictures and later to Paramount. During this time Clara would recollect that she was letting loose and having such a good time that she felt it came through when she was on the screen. Bow became the fixture for the modern woman in the public eye. She would range between a tomboy and flapper on the screen, showing both dichotomies of the era. She would play with sexuality and gender, appealing to a wide audience on the silver screen. Clara Bow would quickly become the face of the silent film era.

The advent of the 'talkies' would take a lot of her colleagues out of the acting game, but it wouldn't stop Clara. She was able to tackle the new sound film genre and remain on top – at least for a time. She pushed herself to be the very best and had a lofty fifty-six film credits to her name by 1931. Clara was so popular at the height of her career, that received over 45,000 fan letters in a single month.

> Clara Bow is the quintessence of what the term 'flapper' signifies ... Pretty, impudent, superbly assured, as world wise, briefly clad and 'hard-berled' as possible. There were hundreds of them – her prototypes. Now, completing the circle, there are thousands more – patterning themselves after her.
>
> F. Scott Fitzgerald, 1927.

Blackmail and Scandal

> The more I see of men, the more I like dogs.
>
> Clara Bow

Clara would employ Daisy De Voe as her personal secretary, needing someone to organise her finances and the chaos of her life at that point. De Voe had taken over Clara's financial wellbeing by 1930. The newspapers caught wind of a scandal before it broke – they discovered that De Voe had been mismanaging Clara's funds and possibly stealing from her. They confronted De Voe for a comment and found that she didn't even know that the story was out: 'As far as I know I am still her secretary. Miss Bow has not served notice on me. I guess I'll have to find out all about it.'

The press went to Clara herself for a comment and she declined to give one. It was only a few days later, however, that Clara fired De Voe. Bow was apparently missing various valuables, like jewellery, rings and money. De Voe attempted to sue Clara and felt that she was owed more money from the star. The district attorney soon had the case on his desk against De Voe:

> This matter came into this office in the nature of a formal request for a criminal complaint against Miss Daisy De Voe for the embezzlement of money and property belonging to Miss Clara Bow. The matter was regularly referred to Mr Blayney Matthews, chief of the bureau of

investigation. After several days of investigation, Mr Matthews reported back that Miss De Voe had made a thirty page confession of the theft of some $35,000 of Miss Bow's money, a great deal of which was found in her possession.

It is the policy of this office that before issuing a complaint against a private citizen to first thoroughly investigate the case in order to prevent a mistake or miscarriage of justice. This investigation was completed today, and this office has no other alternative under the law but to place the matter before the county grand jury.

The case would soon go before a grand jury to see if De Voe would face charges for embezzlement. De Voe wasn't just indicted, she was slammed with a total of thirty-seven counts of grand theft. She stood accused not only of theft of Bow's personal items, but of withdrawing and stealing the modern-day equivalent of hundreds of thousands of dollars.

De Voe reacted to her indictment by filing a complaint of her own against her former employer through her attorney. She claimed that she was owed money for damages by being unlawfully detained while the police investigated the missing property – an act that she maintained that she had not committed. De Voe was seeking the modern equivalent of around $100 thousand in damages.

The attorney for De Voe tried to assault the character of Bow, stating that she overspent money and bought alcohol, which was illegal at the time. Bow insisted that De Voe had control of her checks and money, so if whiskey was purchased, then it was purchased by De Voe for her own purposes. The trial went on to reveal a number of checks signed by Bow that were apparently misused by De Voe for her own personal gain.

De Voe, as it turns out, wasn't the brightest of criminals. She actually admitted to the district attorney in an earlier statement that she had attempted to extort Bow for the modern equivalent of $1.7 million and had taken money from the accounts she should not have, stating that Bow should have been paying attention:

> It was her fault. If she had paid attention to business I wouldn't have taken a dime from her because she would have known about everything. She wouldn't even write her own checks. She put me in a position to take everything I wanted. Of course, I didn't blame her.

The trial was hard on Clara, because De Voe's attorney tried to put her character on trial, which had to be rather upsetting as the victim. The turning point in the trial, however, was when a third-party accountant testified to going through the records and finding a lot more missing money than was originally suspected. When De Voe took the stand to discuss the missing money, she instead proceeded to tell secrets about Clara's personal life. This upset Clara further, causing her to miss parts of the trial due to stress. Her doctor issued the following statement:

> Miss Bow is suffering from a severe cold and from nervous strain attendant on the trial. She is running a temperature and I ordered her to bed.

Her condition is not serious and she should be up
and around in a few days.

The judge would bar any further discussion about Clara's
personal life from the trial. The jury somehow came back
deadlocked and De Voe was sentenced to five years of
probation. She was soon released on bail and continued to
fight her conviction.

The Coast Reporter

What happened next would lead to a very poor year for Clara
Bow. 1931 would prove to be a culmination of many things
that were simply too much for her to handle. A less than
savoury tabloid publisher by the name of Fred H. Girnau
produced four articles about the sexual exploits of Clara
Bow in his trashy paper, called *The Coast Reporter*. The
tabloid printed sensational articles in an expose series about
Bow for four issues, consistently accusing her of lude sexual
behaviour. These were given out door to door, on street
corners and through the mail. The sensational stories made
their rounds enough that the scandal was widespread. The
rumours would get back to Clara and they devastated her.

The vicious rumour and innuendo in *The Coast Reporter*
included accusations that Clara was involved in all sorts of
deviant behaviour, including:

- Having sex in public with her many lovers.
- Travelling to Mexico to gamble. She took a married lover
  there who worked as a dealer at the gambling tables.

She then had a threesome with two prostitutes in front of him. His wife found out, so he killed her and then himself. *The Coast Reporter* made certain to assert that Clara felt no remorse.

- She seduced and had sex with her cousin, Billy Bow.
- She seduced and had sex with her chauffer, Herbert.
- Her sexual appetites were so extreme that when no men were around she would have sex with her female staff.
- If no men or women were around, she would resort to animals, including a koala bear and her dog, Duke.
- Clara was supposedly committed to a hospital, where she was told that she had a social disease. Doctors warned her that her excesses would eventually cause her brain cells to begin disintegration. A suggestion that she is said to have laughed off, saying that she would rather die young and enjoy all of her degenerate desires.

These are only some of the accusations made against Clara. They also made suggestions in the paper that Clara would be better off dead. It was a blatant attack on her character, but why would anyone open themselves up to the trouble that would come with printing false claims? The public assumed that there was truth to these stories. Remember that this was one of the most famous people in the entire world and now everyone believed she was a degenerate. Clara is said to have fled to her dressing room and vomited when she came upon a copy. It wasn't hard to get them, they were being given away outside of the gates of Paramount studios.

This attack wouldn't go unpunished and the man who printed the libellous statements in *The Coast Reporter* would be held accountable in court. Fred H. Girnau would be sentenced for eight years in jail for sending lewd materials through the postal service. Girnau would insist that he got the information from De Voe, who would deny that she gave him permission. The two would end up suing each other.

These events would prove too much for the delicate constitution of Clara and helped lead to her mental breakdown and committal later in 1931.

Clara Suffers a Breakdown

It was on 6 May 1931, and Clara had been pushing herself for nearly a decade. She was partying hard and working even harder. She would have a mental breakdown on the set of a film, smashing a mirror over the head of the director and then attempting to take her own life. The events would lead to her being committed to the Glendale Hospital for the mentally deranged for six months. The 'It' girl had lost it.

She would be released from her Paramount contract during this time. There are some sources that say she requested it – yet others insist that Paramount ditched her for causing too much public drama. Paramount was able to get Clara to sign away the rest of her contract, saving them $60,000 in the process. Regardless of the reasons, Clara was no longer committed to any studio; she felt that her issues stemmed from her intense work, employee betrayal and public sex scandals. These stressful events certainly were likely culprits in the flaring-up of her illness and making things worse for her, but it wasn't something that she could all together escape. Clara learnt later in life that she suffered from a mental illness. Various sources state that she was diagnosed with schizophrenia, though the validity of the diagnosis has been questioned.

Marriage and Legacy

She would meet the love of her life in that same year, a country and western actor by the name of Rex Bell. His calming demeanour was likely a rock for Bow to lean upon and the two would marry in December of 1931, moving out to his ranch in Nevada. They would eventually have two sons and carved out a nice life for themselves, including a run as Lt. Governor of Nevada for Rex. She returned to Hollywood for a two picture deal with Fox in 1932, and then promptly retired from public life. Her nervous condition would continue to plague her throughout her life. In this era, with little relevant assistance for those with anxiety and or mental illness, Clara suffered her life as a 'shut-in' (recluse). Her husband Rex died of a heart attack in 1962, but Clara could not bring herself to attend his funeral. She would, however, attend a second funeral held for him with her children and the public would see her again for the first time in fifteen years.

Clara spent the rest of her days suffering from insomnia and living in and out of sanatoriums. In 1965 she would also die of a heart attack and was laid to rest in Forest Lawn Cemetary, alongside her husband. His inscription reads 'Rex Bell: Lt. Governor State of Nevada. Hers reads 'Clara Bow: Hollywood's 'It' Girl.' Clara has a star on the Hollywood Walk of Fame, which can be found at the East side of the 1500 block of Vine Street.

Bibliography

The Role of Film in Society, 19 June 2011 https://thoughteconomics.com/the-role-of-film-in-society/

A Very Short History of Cinema, 7 January 2011 https://blog.scienceandmediamuseum.org.uk/very-short-history-of-cinema/

History of the Motion Picture, 11 September 2018 https://www.britannica.com/art/history-of-the-motion-picture

Film History by Decade, 2 March 2018 https://www.filmsite.org/filmh.html/1910-filmhistory.html

Bow, Clara (1904–1965), 2002 https://www.encyclopedia.com/women/encyclopedias-almanacs-transcripts-and-maps/bow-clara-1904-1965

Clara Bow and the USC Football Team, 10 August 2007 https://www.snopes.com/fact-check/clara-bow-peep/

The Legacy of Clara Bow, America's First Sex Symbol, 17 May 2018 https://bust.com/movies/16972-the-legacy-of-clara-bow-america-s-first-sex-symbol.html

Epilepsy Foundation: Aggression, 1 October 2018 https://www.epilepsy.com/learn/challenges-epilepsy/moods-and-behaviour/mood-and-behaviour-101/aggression

Clara Bow Has Breakdown, 7 May 1931, *The Barrier Miner*.

TCM, Clara Bow, 2018 http://www.tcm.com/tcmdb/person/ 20150%7C32262/Clara-Bow/

Clara Bow-The Eternal 'It' Girl, 30 March 2018 https:// silentology.wordpress.com/2018/03/30/clara-bow-the- eternal-it-girl/

Stenn, David, *Clara Bow Runnin' Wild*, 1988

Snyder, Sherri, *Barbara LaMarr: The Girl Who Was Too Beautiful for Hollywood*, 2017

Marston, Jack. *Siren Song: The Tragedy of Barbara La Marr*, 2010

IMDB http://www.imdb.com

Mears, Hadley, *The Tragic Story of Barbara La Marr, the Woman who was 'Too Beautiful for Hollywood'*, 10 February 2017 http://www.laweekly.com/arts/the-tragic-story-of- barbara-la-marr-the-woman-who-was-too-beautiful-for- hollywood-7882754

CharlieChaplin.com, 2018. http://www.charliechaplin.com

Encyclopedia Britannica, Charlie Chaplin, 23 August 2018 https://www.britannica.com/biography/Charlie-Chaplin

Brody, Richard. Charlie Chaplin's Scandalous Life and Boundless Artistry, 18 September 2015 https://www. newyorker.com/culture/richard-brody/charlie-chaplins- scandalous-life-and-boundless-artistry

Charlie Chaplin Biography, 5 August 2017 https://www. notablebiographies.com/Ch-Co/Chaplin-Charlie.html

Charlie Chaplin Articles *The Guardian*, 2018 https://www. theguardian.com/film/charliechaplin

E! Mysteries and Scandals Documentary: Joan Crawford

Young Doug Weds Joan, 4 June 1929, *Los Angeles Times*

Johnes, Carl. Joan Crawford: The Last Years. 1979.

Bibliography

Fact-Checking Feud: The Ugly Truth About Joan Crawford and Bette Davis's 1963 Oscar Showdown, 2 April 2017 https://www.vanityfair.com/hollywood/2017/04/fx-feud-joan-crawford-bette-davis-oscars

'Feud:' The Most Shocking Joan Crawford Accusations From 'Mommie Dearest', 17 March 2017 https://www.hollywoodreporter.com/live-feed/mommie-dearest-shocking-joan-crawford-accusations-986654

Joan Crawford's Relationships Spanned Hollywood & Her Career, 12 March 2017 https://www.bustle.com/p/joan-crawfords-relationships-spanned-hollywood-her-career-43268

TCM: Errol Flynn, 2016 http://www.tcm.com/tcmdb/person/63336%7C48996/Errol-Flynn/

Miller, Julie. Errol Flynn's Illicit Romance with a 15-Year-Old, as Remembered by The Last of Robin Hood, 7 September 2013 https://www.vanityfair.com/hollywood/2013/09/errol-flynn-toronto-film-festival

Encyclopedia Britannica: Errol Flynn, 15 November 2018 https://www.britannica.com/biography/Errol-Flynn

Farr, John. The Short and Crazy Life of Errol Flynn, 17 August 2016 https://www.bestmoviesbyfarr.com/articles/errol-flynn-bio/2016/07

Hopper, Tristin. Errol Flynn, warts and all: How the broke Hollywood film star met his end in Vancouver, 18 July 2014 https://nationalpost.com/news/canada/errol-flynn-warts-and-all-how-the-broke-hollywood-film-star-met-his-end-in-vancouver

Tucker, Reed. 5 surprising secrets about Hollywood legend Errol Flynn, 25 August 2014 https://nypost.com/2014/08/25/5-surprising-secrets-about-hollywood-legend-errol-flynn/

Secret Lives: Errol Flynn Documentary. 1996.

'From the archive, 16 October 1959: Hollywood mourns Errol Flynn', 16 October 2013 https://www.theguardian.com/theguardian/2013/oct/16/errol-flynn-death-obituary-actor

Errol Flynn 'worked as a Nazi spy and met Adolf Hitler', 11 July 2009 https://www.telegraph.co.uk/news/worldnews/australiaandthepacific/australia/5799641/Errol-Flynn-worked-as-a-Nazi-spy-and-met-Adolf-Hitler.html

King, Gilbert. The Skinny on the Fatty Arbuckle Trial, 8 November 2011https://www.smithsonianmag.com/history/the-skinny-on-the-fatty-arbuckle-trial-131228859/

Sheerin, Jude. '"Fatty" Arbuckle and Hollywood's first scandal', 4 September 2011 https://www.bbc.com/news/magazine-14640719

History Channel: Jean Harlow Dies, 13 November 2009 https://www.history.com/this-day-in-history/jean-harlow-dies

Hollywood Star Walk http://projects.latimes.com/hollywood/star-walk/

E! Mysteries and Scandals Documentary TV Series: Jean Harlow

E! Mysteries and Scandals Documentary TV Series: Lana Turner

Cheryl Christina Crane Inquest: 1958, 2002 https://www.encyclopedia.com/law/law-magazines/cheryl-christina-crane-inquest-1958

Smith, Doug. In a 1958 inquest, killing of Lana Turner's boyfriend was detailed, 10 August 2015 https://www.latimes.com/local/california/la-me-stompanato-turner-20150810-story.html

Bibliography

E! Mysteries and Scandals Documentary TV Series: Mabel Normand

Fristoe, Roger. TCM: Mickey (1918) http://www.tcm.com/this-month/article/495878%7C0/Mickey.html

Film Stars at Mabel Normand Rites, 3 March 1930, *Chester Times.*

Actress Mae West Sentenced for 'Sex', History.com https://www.historychannel.com.au/articles/actress-mae-west-sentenced-for-sex/

CPI Inflation Calculator https://data.bls.gov/cgi-bin/cpicalc.pl

'Who Was First? The Deiro Brothers Controversy', August 1935, *Accordion News Magazine.*

'Jennings, C. Robert, Mae West: A Candid Conversation with the Queen of Vamp and Camp', January 1971, *Playboy Magazine.*

Watts, Jill, *Mae West: An Icon In Black and White*, Oxford, England: Oxford University Press, 2001

Rich, Frank. Mae West 'Sex' Capade!, 1 April 2012 http://nymag.com/news/features/scandals/mae-west-2012-4/

A New Yorker State of Mind: Mae West https://newyorkerstateofmind.com/tag/mae-west/

PBS: Mae West http://www.pbs.org/wgbh/cultureshock/flashpoints/theater/maewest.html

Mackie, John. This Week in History: 1906 A crazed millionaire shoots a famed architect, 24 June 2016 https://vancouversun.com/news/local-news/this-week-in-history-1906-a-crazed-millionaire-shoots-a-famed-architect

The American Experience: Murder of the Century, Season 8: Episode 1, PBS. 1995.

E! Mysteries and Scandals Documentary TV Series: William Desmond Taylor

Perfect Crimes Documentary, History Channel

Thompson, Emily. A Very Short History of the Transition from Silent to Sound Movies, 2011 https://www.wonderstruckthebook.com/essay_silent-to-sound.htm

'From the Archives: Body of Thelma Todd Found in Death Riddle, 17 December 1935', *LA Times* http://www.latimes.com/local/obituaries/archives/la-me-thelma-todd-19351217-story.html#

Sanello, Frank. MURDER OF '30S STARLET THELMA TODD NO LONGER MYSTERY, 5 May 1991, Chicago Tribune https://www.chicagotribune.com/news/ct-xpm-1991-05-05-9102090725-story.html